GREECE 1

2024

Discover Greece: A Traveler's Guide to Myth, Magic, and Mediterranean Beauty

Sophie Maguire

in this document, including but not limited to - errors, omissions, or inaccuracies.

Table of Contents

Sommario

Introduction

In the azure embrace of the Aegean Sea lies a land of ancient wonders, sun-kissed shores, and timeless allure - Greece. Steeped in mythology, history, and unparalleled natural beauty, Greece beckons travelers from across the globe to immerse themselves in its rich tapestry of culture and landscapes. From the majestic ruins of Athens to the idyllic islands of Santorini and Mykonos, every corner of this enchanting country whispers tales of its glorious past and promises unforgettable experiences in the present.

In the pages of this guide, embark on a voyage of discovery that transcends mere tourism. This meticulously crafted travel guide is your passport to unlocking the secrets of Greece, offering invaluable insights, expert recommendations, and insider tips to ensure your journey is nothing short of extraordinary.

Why Greece? The question echoes through the ages, resonating with the hearts of wanderers and dreamers alike. To answer is to delve into a myriad of reasons that make Greece a must-visit destination for every avid traveler. Firstly, Greece stands as a living museum of civilization, where ancient ruins stand testament to the birthplace of democracy, philosophy, and the arts. From the iconic Acropolis of Athens to the sacred oracle of Delphi, each archaeological site whispers tales of bygone eras, inviting you to trace the footsteps of gods and heroes.

Moreover, Greece's natural beauty is unparalleled. Picture-perfect islands adorned with whitewashed villages cascading down cliffs into crystalline waters, where golden beaches bask under an eternal sun. Whether you seek the vibrant energy of cosmopolitan hubs like Athens and Thessaloniki or the serene tranquility of remote islands like Crete and Zakynthos, Greece offers a diverse array of landscapes to captivate every traveler's soul.

Beyond its historical and natural wonders, Greece enchants with its warm hospitality and vibrant culture. Indulge in the zestful flavors of Mediterranean cuisine, where every bite is a celebration of fresh ingredients and time-honored recipes. Engage in lively conversations with locals over a glass of ouzo or dance to the rhythm of traditional music at a local taverna. In Greece, hospitality isn't just a tradition; it's a way of life, inviting you to become part of the tapestry of Greek culture.

However, navigating the labyrinthine alleys of Greece can be daunting without proper guidance, which is where "Greece Travel Guide 2024' becomes your indispensable companion. More than just a conventional travel guide, this book is a curated collection of experiences, curated by seasoned travelers who have traversed the length and breadth of Greece to bring you the very best it has to offer.

Within its pages, you'll find meticulously researched information on everything from must-visit attractions to off-the-beaten-path gems, ensuring you make the most of your time in Greece. Delve into comprehensive city guides for Athens, Thessaloniki, and beyond, offering detailed insights into the historical significance and modern-day charms of each destination. Whether you're a history buff, a beach lover, a foodie, or an adventure seeker, "Greece Travel Guide 2024'caters to every traveler's interests and preferences.

Moreover, the guide provides practical advice on transportation, accommodation, dining, and safety, empowering you to navigate Greece with confidence and ease. From deciphering Greek menus to mastering basic phrases in the local language, you'll find invaluable tips to enhance your travel experience and immerse yourself fully in Greek culture.

But "Greece Travel Guide 2024 'is more than just a compilation of information; it's a gateway to immersive experiences that will leave an indelible mark on your soul. Discover hidden tavernas where locals gather to savor authentic Greek cuisine, embark on scenic hikes through rugged landscapes dotted with ancient ruins, or set sail on a sunset cruise to uninhabited islands shrouded in myth and legend.

In essence, "Greece Travel Guide 2024' transcends the realm of conventional travel guides to become your trusted companion on a journey of discovery and transformation. Whether you're planning your first trip to Greece or seeking to delve deeper into its wonders, this book is your key to unlocking the secrets of this timeless land. So, pack your bags, prepare to be enchanted, and let "Greece Travel Guide 2024'be your guide to an unforgettable adventure in the cradle of civilization.

Chapter 1: Travel Essentials

Here are ten unique facts about Greece that you should know before visiting:

1. **Birthplace of Democracy:** Greece is widely regarded as the birthplace of democracy, with the ancient city-state of Athens introducing the concept of democratic governance in the 5th century BC. The Athenian democracy allowed citizens to participate in decision-making processes and laid the foundation for modern democratic systems worldwide.

2. **Home of the Olympic Games:** The Olympic Games originated in ancient Greece as a religious festival held in honor of Zeus at Olympia. The first recorded Olympic Games took place in 776 BC, and the tradition continued for over a thousand years until it was revived in its modern form in 1896 in Athens.

3. **Land of Mythology:** Greece is steeped in mythology and ancient lore, with a rich tapestry of gods, heroes, and epic tales that continue to captivate imaginations worldwide. Mount Olympus, the highest mountain in Greece, was believed to be the home of the gods in Greek mythology.

4. **Mediterranean Cuisine:** Greek cuisine is celebrated for its fresh, healthy, and flavorful dishes, influenced by Mediterranean ingredients such as olive oil, herbs, grains, and seafood. Staples of Greek cuisine include

feta cheese, olives, tzatziki, moussaka, souvlaki, and baklava.

5. **Island Paradise:** Greece is renowned for its stunning islands, with over 6,000 islands and islets scattered across the Aegean and Ionian Seas. Each island offers its own unique charm, from the cosmopolitan vibes of Mykonos and Santorini to the tranquil beauty of Crete and Corfu.

6. **Ancient Ruins:** Greece is home to some of the most well-preserved ancient ruins and archaeological sites in the world, including the Acropolis of Athens, the Temple of Apollo at Delphi, the Palace of Knossos in Crete, and the ancient theater of Epidaurus.

7. **Blue Flag Beaches:** Greece boasts some of the cleanest and most beautiful beaches in Europe, with over 400 beaches awarded the prestigious Blue Flag designation for their water quality, cleanliness, and environmental management.

8. **Philosophical Legacy:** Greece is renowned for its contributions to philosophy, with ancient Greek philosophers such as Socrates, Plato, and Aristotle laying the groundwork for Western philosophy and intellectual thought. Their ideas continue to influence fields such as ethics, logic, and metaphysics.

9. **Orthodox Christianity:** The majority of Greeks belong to the Greek Orthodox Church, which plays a significant role in Greek culture, traditions, and

religious practices. Greek Orthodox Christianity has deep roots in Greece, with Byzantine-era churches and monasteries dotting the landscape.

10. **Warm Hospitality:** Greeks are known for their warm hospitality and philoxenia, or love of strangers, welcoming visitors with open arms and generous hospitality. Sharing food, conversation, and camaraderie is an integral part of Greek culture, making visitors feel welcome and embraced.

These unique facts about Greece provide a glimpse into the country's rich history, culture, and natural beauty, offering travelers a deeper understanding and appreciation of this fascinating destination.

Before traveling to Greece, here are some important things you should know:

Best Time To Visit Greece

The best time to visit Greece depends on various factors such as cost, weather, and crowds, each of which can significantly impact your travel experience. Let's explore these factors in detail:

1. Cost:

- Off-peak seasons, typically during the shoulder months of April to May and September to October, often offer the best value for money in Greece. During these periods, you can find more affordable accommodation options, cheaper flights, and reduced rates for tours and activities.

- Avoiding peak tourist seasons, such as the summer months of June to August, can help you save significantly on expenses. Prices tend to skyrocket during these months due to high demand, especially in popular tourist destinations like Santorini and Mykonos.

2. Seasons:

- Spring (April to May): Spring is an ideal time to visit Greece, as the weather is pleasantly warm, and the landscapes are adorned with blooming flowers. Temperatures are mild, ranging from around 15°C to 25°C (59°F to 77°F) on average, making it perfect for exploring historical sites and hiking trails without the scorching heat of summer.

- Autumn (September to October): Autumn offers similar advantages to spring, with mild temperatures and fewer crowds. The sea remains warm for swimming, and the autumnal colors add a picturesque charm to the landscapes. It's an excellent time for cultural festivals and wine tasting tours in regions like the Peloponnese and Crete.

3. Crowds:

- Peak Season (June to August): Summer is the busiest time in Greece, with tourists flocking to the islands and coastal areas to enjoy the sun, sea, and vibrant nightlife. While the weather is hot and sunny, popular destinations can become overcrowded, leading to long queues at attractions, congested beaches, and higher prices.

- Shoulder Season (April to May, September to October): The shoulder months offer a perfect balance between favorable weather conditions and fewer crowds. You can still enjoy warm temperatures and sunshine while avoiding the peak tourist rush. Attractions are less crowded, allowing for a more relaxed and authentic travel experience.

Considering these factors, the optimal time to visit Greece would be during the shoulder seasons of spring (April to May) and autumn (September to October). Not only will you enjoy pleasant weather and fewer crowds, but you'll also have the opportunity to explore Greece's treasures without breaking the bank. Whether you're seeking cultural immersion, outdoor adventures, or simply relaxation by the Mediterranean, Greece welcomes you with open arms year-round, but the shoulder seasons offer a particularly enticing blend of affordability, pleasant weather, and tranquility.

What to pack

Packing for a trip to Greece requires consideration of the country's diverse landscapes, weather conditions, and cultural activities. Here's a comprehensive packing list to ensure you're well-prepared for your Greek adventure:

1. **Clothing:**

   - Lightweight, breathable clothing: Pack comfortable shirts, shorts, dresses, and skirts for hot summer days.

   - Light layers: Bring a light sweater or jacket for cooler evenings, especially in spring and autumn.

   - Swimwear: Don't forget your swimsuit for beach days or lounging by the pool.

   - Comfortable walking shoes: Choose sturdy sandals or walking shoes for exploring ancient ruins, cobblestone streets, and hiking trails.

   - Hat and sunglasses: Protect yourself from the sun with a wide-brimmed hat and UV-blocking sunglasses.

- Beach cover-up: A sarong or light cover-up is handy for transitioning from the beach to cafes or restaurants.

- Casual evening wear: Pack a few dressier outfits for dining out or enjoying nightlife in cities like Athens or Thessaloniki.

2. **Accessories:**

- Daypack or tote bag: Carry a lightweight bag for daily excursions, sightseeing, and beach outings.

- Travel-sized umbrella or rain jacket: While Greece is known for its sunny weather, occasional rain showers can occur, especially in spring and autumn.

- Travel adapter and portable charger: Ensure you can charge your devices and stay connected while exploring Greece.

- Reusable water bottle: Stay hydrated, especially during hot summer days, by carrying a refillable water bottle.

- Camera or smartphone: Capture memories of Greece's stunning landscapes, ancient ruins, and vibrant culture.

3. **Toiletries and Personal Care:**

- Sunscreen: Protect your skin from the strong Mediterranean sun with a high SPF sunscreen.

- Insect repellent: Ward off mosquitoes, especially if you're visiting rural areas or during the evening.

- Personal hygiene items: Pack essentials like toothbrush, toothpaste, shampoo, conditioner, and any prescription medications.

- Travel-sized toiletries: Opt for travel-sized bottles of shampoo, conditioner, and body wash to save space in your luggage.

4. **Documents and Essentials:**

- Passport and travel documents: Ensure you have a valid passport, visa (if required), travel insurance, and any necessary reservations or tickets.

- Cash and credit cards: Bring a mix of cash (in euros) and credit cards for purchases, dining, and emergencies.

- Guidebook or travel apps: Carry a Greece travel guide or download relevant travel apps for maps, language translation, and local recommendations.

- Copies of important documents: Keep photocopies or digital copies of your passport, travel insurance, and itinerary in case of loss or theft.

5. **Optional Items:**

- Snorkeling gear: If you plan to explore Greece's underwater world, consider packing snorkeling equipment.

- Travel journal: Capture your thoughts, experiences, and memories in a travel journal or notebook.

- Portable first aid kit: Pack basic medical supplies like bandages, pain relievers, antiseptic wipes, and motion sickness medication.

By packing smartly and considering the activities and weather conditions you'll encounter during your trip, you can ensure a comfortable and enjoyable stay in Greece. Don't forget to leave some space in your luggage for souvenirs and treasures collected along the way!

Getting there and moving around

Getting to Greece and moving around within the country involves various transportation options, each offering its own advantages depending on your itinerary and preferences. Here's a guide to getting there and navigating Greece:

1. **By Air:**

   - International flights: Greece is served by several international airports, with Athens International Airport (ATH) being the largest and busiest. Other major airports include Thessaloniki

Airport (SKG), Heraklion Airport (HER) on Crete, and Rhodes Airport (RHO).

- Domestic flights: Domestic air travel is convenient for traveling between major cities and islands. Greek airlines like Aegean Airlines and Olympic Air operate frequent flights connecting Athens with popular destinations such as Santorini, Mykonos, and Crete.

2. **By Sea:**

- Ferries: Greece boasts an extensive network of ferries, connecting mainland ports with islands throughout the Aegean and Ionian Seas. Ferries range from high-speed catamarans to slower, traditional vessels, offering a range of options to suit different budgets and preferences. Piraeus Port in Athens is the main hub for ferry services, with routes to islands like Santorini, Mykonos, and Naxos.

- Cruises: Many cruise lines offer Mediterranean itineraries that include stops in Greek ports. Cruising allows you to explore multiple destinations in Greece and other Mediterranean countries while enjoying onboard amenities and entertainment.

3. **By Land:**

- Public transportation: Greece has an extensive network of buses and trains connecting major cities and towns. KTEL buses are the primary mode of intercity travel, while trains operated by TrainOSE serve certain routes, including the Athens-Thessaloniki line. Public transportation is affordable and convenient for traveling within mainland Greece.

- Car rental: Renting a car gives you the flexibility to explore Greece at your own pace, especially if you plan to visit remote areas or off-the-beaten-path destinations. Major car rental companies have offices at airports and in city centers, offering a range of vehicles to suit your needs.

4. **Local Transportation:**

- Taxis: Taxis are readily available in Greek cities and tourist areas. It's advisable to use official taxi stands or reputable taxi-hailing apps to ensure fair pricing and avoid scams.

- Public transit: Major cities like Athens and Thessaloniki have efficient public transit systems, including buses, metro, and trams. Purchasing a reloadable transportation card or individual tickets allows for easy access to public transit options.

Navigating Greece's transportation network may seem daunting at first, but with careful planning and a sense of adventure, you'll soon discover the joys of exploring this captivating country by air, sea, and land. Whether you're island-hopping in the Aegean, traversing ancient pathways on the mainland, or cruising along the Mediterranean coast, Greece offers endless opportunities for memorable travel experiences.

Practical information for visitors

Language and communication

Language and communication in Greece are an integral part of the travel experience, as they facilitate interactions with locals, enhance cultural immersion, and ensure smooth navigation through various situations. Here's what you need to know about language and communication in Greece:

1. **Official Language:** The official language of Greece is Greek (Elliniká), which is spoken by the majority of the population. Greek belongs to the Hellenic branch of the Indo-European language family and has a rich history dating back thousands of years.

2. **English Proficiency:** English is widely spoken in tourist areas, major cities, and among younger generations in Greece. Most people working in the tourism industry, such as hotel staff, tour guides, and restaurant employees, have at least a basic understanding of English. However, proficiency levels may vary, especially in rural or remote areas.

3. **Basic Greek Phrases:**

- Learning a few basic Greek phrases can enhance your travel experience and demonstrate respect for the local culture. Here are some essential phrases to know:

  - Hello: Γεια σας (Yia sas)

  - Thank you: Ευχαριστώ (Efharistó)

  - Please: Παρακαλώ (Parakaló)

  - Yes: Ναι (Ne)

  - No: Όχι (Óchi)

  - Excuse me: Συγνώμη (Sygnómi)

  - Goodbye: Αντίο (Adió)

4. **Language Apps and Resources:**

   - Language learning apps like Duolingo, Rosetta Stone, and Babbel offer Greek courses that can help you learn basic vocabulary and phrases before your trip.

   - Travel phrasebooks and pocket dictionaries are useful for quick reference and communication in various situations, especially if you encounter language barriers.

5. **Nonverbal Communication:**

   - Nonverbal cues such as gestures, facial expressions, and body language play a significant role in communication in Greece. Greeks are known for their expressive gestures and warm demeanor, which can help bridge language gaps and facilitate understanding.

- When communicating with locals, maintain eye contact, smile, and be respectful of cultural norms regarding personal space and interactions.

6. **Cultural Sensitivity:**

- Demonstrating cultural sensitivity and respect for Greek customs and traditions fosters positive interactions with locals. Taking the time to learn about Greek etiquette, greetings, and social norms can enhance your communication and cultural immersion experience.

Overall, while Greek is the primary language in Greece, English proficiency is widespread, especially in tourist areas. However, making an effort to learn basic Greek phrases and understanding cultural nuances can enrich your travel experience and foster meaningful connections with locals. Communication is not just about language; it's about building bridges, sharing experiences, and embracing cultural diversity.

Currency And Banking

Understanding the currency and banking system in Greece is essential for managing your finances and transactions during your travels. Here's a guide to currency and banking in Greece:

1. **Currency:**

   - The official currency of Greece is the Euro (EUR), abbreviated as €. Euro banknotes come in denominations of €5, €10, €20, €50, €100, €200, and €500, while coins come in denominations of 1, 2, 5, 10, 20, and 50 cents, as well as €1 and €2.

   - It's advisable to carry a mix of cash and credit/debit cards for different types of transactions and emergencies. Many establishments in Greece accept credit and debit cards, but it's always wise to have some cash on hand, especially in smaller towns or when visiting local markets or tavernas.

2. **ATMs (Automated Teller Machines):**

   - ATMs are widely available throughout Greece, especially in urban areas, tourist destinations, and major cities. They can be found at banks, airports, train stations, shopping centers, and convenience stores.

   - Most ATMs in Greece offer instructions and transaction options in multiple languages, including English. However, it's a good idea to inform your bank of your travel plans before departing to ensure that your cards will work abroad without any issues.

- Withdrawals from ATMs may incur fees, including foreign transaction fees charged by your bank. Check with your bank for information on fees and withdrawal limits to avoid unexpected charges.

3. **Credit and Debit Cards:**

- Credit and debit cards are widely accepted in Greece, especially in urban areas, hotels, restaurants, and larger retail stores. Visa and Mastercard are the most commonly accepted card networks, followed by American Express and Diners Club, though acceptance may vary.

- When using your credit or debit card for purchases, you may be asked to present identification (e.g., passport) for security purposes. Contactless payments (tap-and-go) are becoming increasingly common in Greece, especially for smaller transactions.

4. **Currency Exchange:**

- Currency exchange services are available at banks, exchange offices (often labeled as "Foreign Exchange" or "Forex"), airports, and major tourist areas. While exchanging currency at airports or tourist hotspots may be convenient, rates may be less favorable compared to banks or official exchange offices.

- It's advisable to exchange only the amount of cash you need for immediate expenses, as you may receive better exchange rates or lower fees from ATMs or credit/debit card transactions.

5. **Banking Hours:**

- Banks in Greece typically operate from Monday to Friday, with varying hours depending on the location and branch. Most banks are open from around 8:00 or 8:30 AM to 2:30 or 3:00 PM. Some branches may offer extended hours on select days or during peak tourist seasons.

- Keep in mind that banking hours may be reduced on Saturdays or during public holidays, so it's best to plan your banking needs accordingly.

By familiarizing yourself with the currency and banking system in Greece, you can manage your finances effectively and enjoy a seamless travel experience without any financial surprises. Whether you're withdrawing cash from ATMs, using credit cards for purchases, or exchanging currency, being prepared ensures that you can focus on enjoying your time exploring Greece's vibrant culture, stunning landscapes, and rich history.

Safety

Ensuring your safety while traveling in Greece is essential for a worry-free and enjoyable experience. Here are some tips to help you stay safe during your visit:

1. **General Safety Precautions:**

   - Stay aware of your surroundings, especially in crowded tourist areas, markets, and public transportation hubs where pickpocketing may occur.

   - Keep your belongings secure by using anti-theft bags, money belts, or hidden pouches to store valuables such as passports, cash, and electronics.

   - Be cautious when interacting with strangers, especially if approached by individuals offering unsolicited services or assistance.

   - Avoid walking alone in poorly lit or unfamiliar areas, especially at night. Stick to well-lit streets and populated areas, and consider using reputable transportation services like taxis or rideshare apps after dark.

   - Familiarize yourself with local laws, customs, and emergency contact information, including the nearest embassy or consulate for your country.

2. **Health and Safety Precautions:**

- Stay hydrated, especially during hot summer months, by drinking plenty of water and avoiding prolonged exposure to direct sunlight.

- Use sunscreen with a high SPF to protect your skin from harmful UV rays, and wear hats, sunglasses, and lightweight clothing to shield yourself from the sun.

- Practice good hygiene habits, including frequent handwashing and using hand sanitizer, to prevent the spread of illness, especially during flu seasons or outbreaks.

- Carry any necessary medications, including prescription medications, in their original packaging with clear labels to avoid any issues with customs or medical emergencies.

3. **Transportation Safety:**

- Choose reputable transportation providers and adhere to safety guidelines when using taxis, buses, trains, or ferries. Verify the legitimacy of taxis by ensuring they have official markings, meters, and identification displayed prominently.

- Follow safety instructions and regulations when participating in recreational activities such as water sports, hiking, or adventure tours. Wear appropriate safety gear and avoid taking unnecessary risks, especially in unfamiliar or hazardous environments.

4. **Natural Disaster Preparedness:**

- Greece is prone to natural disasters such as earthquakes, wildfires, and occasional severe weather events. Stay informed about potential risks and follow guidance from local authorities and emergency services in the event of an emergency.

- Familiarize yourself with evacuation procedures, emergency shelter locations, and communication channels for receiving updates and alerts from official sources.

5. **Emergency Contacts:**

- Memorize or keep a written list of emergency contact numbers, including local emergency services (police, fire, medical), your embassy or consulate, and travel insurance providers. It's also a good idea to have a mobile phone with international roaming or a local SIM card for making emergency calls.

By staying vigilant, informed, and prepared, you can mitigate potential risks and enjoy a safe and rewarding travel experience in Greece. Remember to trust your instincts, prioritize your well-being, and take necessary precautions to ensure a memorable and worry-free trip.

Chapter 2: Must Visit Places in Greece

Greece, located in southeastern Europe, occupies the southernmost tip of the Balkan Peninsula and is surrounded by the Ionian Sea to the west, the Mediterranean Sea to the south, and the Aegean Sea to the east. Its geographical features are diverse and captivating, ranging from mountainous terrain to coastal plains and idyllic islands.

1. **Mainland Greece:** The mainland of Greece is characterized by rugged mountain ranges, including the Pindus Range in the north and the Taygetus Range in the south. The central region is dominated by the Attica Peninsula, home to the capital city, Athens, and the historic region of Attica.

2. **Peloponnese Peninsula:** Connected to the mainland by the Isthmus of Corinth, the Peloponnese Peninsula is a land of ancient history and natural beauty. It is home to iconic landmarks such as the ancient city of Olympia, the fortified town of Mycenae, and the UNESCO World Heritage Site of Mystras.

3. **Islands of the Aegean:** Greece boasts over 6,000 islands and islets scattered across the Aegean Sea, each with its own unique charm and character. The Cyclades islands, including Mykonos, Santorini, and Paros, are famous for their whitewashed buildings, blue-domed churches, and stunning sunsets. The Dodecanese

islands, such as Rhodes and Kos, offer a blend of ancient history and vibrant culture, while the Sporades islands, including Skiathos and Skopelos, are known for their lush green landscapes and crystal-clear waters.

4. **Ionian Islands:** Located off the western coast of Greece, the Ionian Islands are renowned for their lush vegetation, sandy beaches, and emerald waters. Corfu, the largest of the Ionian islands, boasts Venetian architecture, Byzantine churches, and picturesque villages. Kefalonia, known for its dramatic coastline and underground caves, inspired the novel and film "Captain Corelli's Mandolin."

5. **Crete:** The largest island in Greece, Crete, lies in the southern Aegean Sea and is known for its diverse landscapes, ranging from rugged mountains and fertile plains to palm-fringed beaches and ancient ruins. Crete is steeped in mythology and history, with legendary sites such as the Palace of Knossos, the birthplace of Zeus at Mount Ida, and the Samaria Gorge.

6. **Coastal Plains:** Along Greece's coastline, you'll find fertile coastal plains ideal for agriculture and tourism. These plains are dotted with olive groves, vineyards, and citrus orchards, producing some of the finest olive oil, wine, and citrus fruits in the world.

7. **Mediterranean Climate:** Greece enjoys a Mediterranean climate with hot, dry summers and mild, wet winters. The country experiences ample

sunshine throughout the year, making it an ideal destination for outdoor activities, beach holidays, and cultural exploration.

Here are ten compelling reasons why Greece should be at the top of your travel bucket list:

1. Ancient History and Archaeological Sites: Greece is the cradle of Western civilization, boasting a rich history that spans thousands of years. Explore iconic archaeological sites such as the Acropolis of Athens, the ancient city of Delphi, and the ruins of Olympia, where the first Olympic Games were held.

2. Stunning Islands and Beaches: Greece is home to over 6,000 islands and islets scattered across the Aegean and Ionian Seas. From the dramatic cliffs of Santorini to the pristine beaches of Mykonos and the turquoise waters of Crete, each island offers its own unique charm and beauty.

3. Legendary Hospitality: Experience Greek hospitality firsthand as you immerse yourself in the warmth and generosity of the locals. From family-owned tavernas serving traditional cuisine to lively celebrations of music and dance, Greeks welcome visitors with open arms and a zest for life.

4. Mouthwatering Cuisine: Indulge in the flavors of the Mediterranean with Greece's renowned cuisine, featuring fresh seafood, olive oil, herbs, and locally sourced ingredients. Sample classic dishes such as

moussaka, souvlaki, Greek salad, and baklava, accompanied by a glass of ouzo or tsipouro.

5. Breathtaking Landscapes: From rugged mountains to fertile valleys, Greece's diverse landscapes offer endless opportunities for outdoor adventures. Hike through gorges, swim in crystal-clear waters, or take a scenic drive along coastal roads lined with olive groves and vineyards.

6. Timeless Architecture: Marvel at Greece's architectural wonders, from ancient temples and Byzantine churches to neoclassical mansions and Venetian fortresses. Explore the narrow streets of old towns like Rhodes and Corfu, where every corner tells a story of the past.

7. Vibrant Cultural Festivals: Experience Greece's vibrant cultural traditions through festivals, celebrations, and events held throughout the year. From religious feasts and folklore festivals to music concerts and theater performances, there's always something happening to celebrate life and community.

8. Mythology and Legends: Delve into the realm of Greek mythology and legends as you visit sites associated with ancient gods and heroes. Walk in the footsteps of Odysseus at Ithaca, visit the birthplace of Zeus at Mount Olympus, or explore the labyrinth of the Minotaur at Knossos.

9. Spectacular Sunsets: Witness some of the most breathtaking sunsets in the world from Greece's

picturesque islands and coastal villages. Whether you're watching the sun dip below the horizon in Santorini's caldera or painting the sky with hues of pink and orange in Mykonos, each sunset is a magical experience.

10. Soul-Stirring Sunrises: Start your day with a sunrise over the Aegean Sea, casting a golden glow over ancient ruins and tranquil landscapes. Whether you're practicing yoga on the beach, hiking to hilltop monasteries, or sipping coffee on a terrace overlooking the sea, the sunrise in Greece is a moment of pure beauty and inspiration.

From its ancient heritage and stunning scenery to its vibrant culture and legendary hospitality, Greece offers a travel experience like no other. Whether you're seeking relaxation, adventure, or cultural immersion, Greece welcomes you with open arms and promises memories that will last a lifetime.

Here are top destinations`;

1.Athens

Greece's capital city, Athens, is a fascinating place to visit since it combines ancient history with contemporary metropolitan activity. Here are some interesting facts about Athens along with its well-known tourist attractions and enticing attractions:

- Athens is one of the world's oldest cities, having a long history dating back more than 3,000 years. It is often considered as the origin of Western culture and the birthplace of democracy.

- Acropolis: Perched atop a rocky outcrop above the city, the Acropolis is a famous ancient citadel. The Parthenon, the Erechtheion, and the Temple of Athena Nike are just a few of the well-known buildings that call this city home. A must-see sight, the Acropolis provides stunning vistas of Athens.

- Parthenon: The Parthenon is a historic temple devoted to the goddess Athena that is located atop the Acropolis. It is a work of art in architecture and a persisting representation of ancient Greece. Visitors can wander the ruins and see the famed structure's unique detailing.

- Athens' Plaka is a lovely district distinguished by its winding, serpentine lanes, neoclassical structures, and lively atmosphere. By way of its classic Greek tavernas, gift shops, and scenic courtyards, it provides an insight into the city's past. It seems like traveling back in time to explore Plaka.

- National Archaeological Museum: The National Archaeological Museum is a must-see location for history buffs. It contains a sizable collection of ancient Greek items, including jewelry, ceramics, sculptures, and relics from many Greek archaeological sites.

- The Ancient Agora, which served as a market, political hub, and gathering spot, was the core of ancient Athens. Today, tourists can explore the remains and go to the Stoa of Attalos, an old structure that currently serves as a museum with Agora relics on show.

- Modern City Life: Athens is a bustling, modern city that is nonetheless steeped in history. Visitors can take in the city's busy nightlife and culinary options, explore trendy neighborhoods like Exarcheia and Koukaki, or enjoy the city's flourishing street art scene.

- Athens Riviera: Conveniently located in the city center, the Athens Riviera is home to stunning beaches, opulent resorts, and waterfront dining. Visitors can take advantage of the water activities available, relax by the beautiful waters, or stroll down the promenade while taking in the breathtaking views of the Aegean Sea.

- Greek Cuisine: With its extensive selection of traditional Greek dishes and foreign cuisine, Athens is a food lover's heaven. Visitors can take a culinary tour of Athens that includes souvlaki, moussaka, fresh seafood, and delectable pastries.

- Greeks are renowned for their friendly and cordial hospitality. Friendly residents willing to share their culture and assist visitors in making the most of their stay are to be expected in Athens.

2. Thessaloniki

The second-largest city in Greece is Thessaloniki. It is a dynamic city with a deep history, a wide range of cultures, and many attractions that make it a well-liked travel destination. Here are some essential details about Thessaloniki and its top attractions that lure tourists from all over the world:

- Thessaloniki has a fascinating history that spans more than 2,300 years, which is of historical significance. It was established in 315 BC and given the name Thessaloniki by Cassander, an Alexander the Great general. Numerous civilizations have had an impact on the city over the course of its history, including the Romans, Byzantines, Ottomans, and more, leaving behind a variety of historical sites.

- UNESCO World Heritage Sites: There are a number of UNESCO World Heritage Sites in Thessaloniki that history buffs must see. Thessaloniki's Paleochristian and Byzantine Monuments contain well-known structures like the Church of Agios Dimitrios, the Galerius Rotunda, and the Galerius Arch.

- White Tower: The White Tower is Thessaloniki's most recognizable landmark. This cylindrical tower, which was constructed during the Ottoman era, stands tall on the seafront and provides sweeping views of the city and the Thermaic Gulf. There is a museum that displays Thessaloniki's history inside the tower.

- Aristotelous Square: Thessaloniki's main square and a popular gathering spot, Aristotelous Square. It is the center of the social and cultural life of the city and is lined with cafes, boutiques, and stunning neoclassical structures. Visitors can take a leisurely stroll, observe locals, or indulge in nearby food and shopping.

- Ano Poli (Upper Town): Perched on a hill with a view of the city, Ano Poli is Thessaloniki's historic center. It is a lovely area with tiny cobblestone lanes, classic homes, and walls from the Byzantine era. Visitors can visit ancient sites like the Trigoniou Tower and the Church of Osios David while exploring Ano Poli to get a sense of the city's past.

- Museums: Thessaloniki is home to a wide range of museums that serve a range of interests. Thessaloniki's Archaeological Museum is home to a sizable collection of ancient Macedonian artifacts, including magnificent gold jewels. The Museum of Byzantine Culture, the Museum of the Macedonian Struggle, and the Museum of Modern Art are a few further noteworthy institutions.

- Dynamic Nightlife: Thessaloniki is well known for having a dynamic nightlife. Trendy pubs, clubs, live music venues, and classic taverns are just a few of the city's entertainment offerings. Particularly well-liked for its bustling ambiance and superb dining options, the lively Ladadika neighborhood.

- Festivals & Events: Throughout the year, Thessaloniki is home to a number of festivals and events. One of the most esteemed film festivals in Southeast Europe is the

Thessaloniki International Film Festival, which takes place every November. The Dimitria Festival, which honors the patron saint of the city, features theater productions, concerts, and exhibitions.

- Thessaloniki offers a wonderful culinary scene, making it a delight for food aficionados. The city is renowned for its scrumptious souvlaki, bougatsa (a classic pastry), and the regional beverage known as tsipouro. It is possible to sample local specialties and fresh products by exploring the city's marketplaces, like Modiano and Kapani.

- Distance from Other Attractions: Thessaloniki is a great starting point for visiting other alluring locations in Northern Greece. The archaeological site of Vergina, where the tomb of Philip II (Alexander the Great's father) was found, and Mount Olympus, the fabled abode of the ancient Greek gods, are two nearby attractions.

3.Santorini

Greece's gorgeous island of Santorini is part of the Aegean Sea and is renowned for its extraordinary scenery, breathtaking views, and fascinating past. Following are some interesting facts about Santorini, along with travel recommendations and the island's top attractions:

- Geological Wonder: The crescent-shaped shape of Santorini was created by a volcanic explosion that took place about 3,600 years ago. One of Santorini's distinguishing characteristics, the caldera is a sizable volcanic crater that offers breathtaking views.

- Beautiful scenery: The island is well-known for its charming whitewashed structures, blue-domed churches, and winding, little lanes. A magnificent and recognizable scene is produced by the buildings' strikingly different colors and the azure water.

- Stunning Sunsets: Santorini is well known for its captivating sunsets. The settlement of Oia, positioned on the island's northernmost point, is well-known for its stunning views of the setting sun over the Aegean Sea.

- Beautiful Beaches: Santorini is home to distinctive beaches with breathtaking scenery. The most well-liked options include Red Beach, distinguished by its reddish cliffs, and Perissa Beach, distinguished by its black volcanic sand. Tourists also adore the beaches of Kamari and Perivolos.

- Visitors can tour historical landmarks and ancient ruins on the island, which is rich in history. The "Minoan Pompeii" is a term that is frequently used to refer to Akrotiri, a Bronze Age settlement that has been preserved by volcanic ash. On a mountaintop, Ancient Thera's remains provide sweeping views.

- Local Food and Wine: Santorini is well known for its mouthwatering cuisine and distinctive regional products. The peculiar flavors of the island's fruits, vegetables, and wines are a result of the soil's volcanic composition. Don't pass up the chance to sample Assyrtiko, a well-known local white wine.

- Destination for Romance: Santorini is frequently considered as one of the world's most romantic locations. It is a popular destination for honeymooners and couples because of its gorgeous scenery, opulent accommodations, and cozy atmosphere.

- Adventure and Activities: Visitors can partake in a number of activities in addition to admiring the island's natural beauty. Take a sailing cruise around the caldera or go scuba diving to see the underwater ecosystem. Hikers can take use of beautiful pathways like the Fira to Oia path.

- Santorini is filled with lovely towns that are worth exploring. Villages like Imerovigli, Pyrgos, and Megalochori, in addition to Oia and Fira (the capital), provide an insight into the island's traditional way of life and boast breathtaking vistas.

- Greek hospitality is renowned worldwide, and Santorini is no exception. The island's rich cultural legacy and the friendly and hospitable residents all add up to an amazing experience.

4.Meteora Monasteries

The Meteora Monasteries are an extraordinary and inspiring location that draws visitors from all over the world to central Greece, close to the town of Kalambaka. Here are some details on the Meteora Monasteries and some of the factors that make them so popular with tourists.:

- The Meteora Monasteries are highly significant from a religious and historical standpoint. They were initially constructed by Orthodox monks who desired seclusion and seclusion in the 14th and 15th centuries. During a period of political unrest, the monasteries acted as refuges for the soul and as educational institutions.

- Meteora Monasteries are a UNESCO World Heritage Site, honored for its historic relevance, architectural brilliance, and magnificent natural beauty.

- Beautiful Location: The Meteora Monasteries are distinguished by their beautiful location. They are placed on enormous granite pillars, which produces an incredible and dramatic scene. With their distinctive shapes and sizes, the rocks' geological formation is a sight to behold.

- Visitors to the Meteora Monasteries can learn about the history and manner of life of the monks. Some monasteries are still in use today, housing monks and nuns who live and practice their religion there. The religious items, manuscripts, and works of art housed in the monasteries' museums provide a window into their rich past.

- Panoramic Views and Photography Opportunities: The monasteries offer truly stunning panoramic views. Visitors can take in expansive views of the Pindus

Mountains, cliffs, and neighboring valleys. For those who enjoy taking photographs, Meteora is a photographer's dream.

- Hiking and nature exploration: Meteora has amazing outdoor recreation and nature exploration opportunities. Visitors can get a close-up view of the area's splendor on the hiking paths. Visitors can see uncommon species of birds as they stroll along the picturesque walkways and take in the distinctive flora and fauna.

- Cultural and Architectural Wonder: The monastery' architecture is remarkable in and of itself. The buildings, which were built on top of the rocks, mix in well with the surroundings. The excellent Byzantine art and workmanship of the time are displayed in the frescoes and interior decorations.

- Film and Pop Culture Connections: A number of films, including the James Bond film "For Your Eyes Only," have included scenes from the Meteora Monasteries. The monasteries' fame has also been increased by the fact that they serve as the iconic background for various music videos, documentaries, and travel-related television programs.

- Guided Excursions & Experiences: Guests can join guided tours to see the monasteries and discover their spiritual significance as well as their history. In-depth explanations of the monastic way of life and local tales are given by knowledgeable guides.

- Peace and Serenity: The Meteora Monasteries provide a tranquil and calm setting. The remote area is surrounded by nature and offers a respite from the busyness of modern life. The serene atmosphere of the monasteries serves as a source of comfort and spiritual inspiration for many tourists.

Visiting the Meteora Monasteries is a unique experience that combines history, spirituality, natural beauty, and cultural exploration. It's no wonder that they attract countless tourists who are captivated by their mystical charm and breathtaking setting.

5.Mykonos

A well-liked tourist resort in Greece's Cyclades islands is Mykonos. Mykonos draws tourists from all over the world because of its exciting nightlife, gorgeous beaches, and endearing traditional architecture. The following are some important details about Mykonos and its top attractions:

- Gorgeous Beaches: Mykonos is renowned for its gorgeous beaches with blue waves and golden sand. Paradise Beach, Super Paradise Beach, Psarou Beach, and Platis Gialos are a few of the most well-known beaches. These beaches include a wide range of water sports, beach clubs, and breathtaking sunset views.

- Charming Mykonos Town, commonly referred to as Chora or Mykonos Town, is the island's capital and is a charming maze of winding alleyways, whitewashed structures, and brightly colored doors and window frames. Its attractiveness is enhanced by the town's famous windmills. The town's abundance of specialty stores, galleries, cafes, and restaurants contributes to its dynamic and colorful atmosphere.

- Little Venice: Little Venice is a district in Mykonos Town that provides breathtaking ocean views. Buildings in this area are constructed close next to the ocean, and some even have balconies that overlook the water. It's a well-liked location to enjoy a meal or beverage while taking in the stunning sunset.

- Delos Island: Delos is a small island with significant historical and archaeological interest that is only a short boat journey from Mykonos. It is a UNESCO World Heritage Site and regarded as one of Greece's most significant archaeological sites. Visitors can explore ancient ruins in Delos, including temples, homes, and statues, which is thought to be the location of the birthplaces of Apollo and Artemis.

- Dynamic Nightlife: Mykonos is well known for its exciting and vivacious nightlife. The island is home to a large number of nightclubs, bars, and beach clubs that host events and provide entertainment all night long. Famous nightlife locations include Scandinavian Bar, Cavo Paradiso, and Paradise Club.

- Water Sports and Activities: Mykonos caters to adventure seekers with a variety of water sports and activities. Jet skiing, windsurfing, paddleboarding, scuba diving, and snorkeling are among the activities you can enjoy. There are places to rent gear and take lessons on several beaches.

- Cosmopolitan Ambiance: Mykonos boasts a hip and cosmopolitan atmosphere that draws international celebrities, fashionistas, and artists. Throughout the year, it organizes a variety of cultural events, art exhibits, and music festivals, enhancing its appeal as a hip destination.

- Gourmet Dining: Mykonos has a thriving restaurant and taverna scene offering a variety of Greek and international cuisines. Visitors can enjoy a variety of delectable gastronomic experiences, from traditional Greek cuisine to gourmet fusion concoctions.

- Luxury Accommodations: There are many different types of accommodations available on Mykonos, including boutique hotels, luxury resorts, and lovely villas. Many accommodations provide breathtaking Aegean Sea views, private pools, and upscale amenities to guarantee a relaxing and opulent stay.

- Mykonos has a long history of being regarded as an LGBT-friendly vacation spot. It boasts a thriving LGBT scene with gay-friendly pubs, clubs, and events, especially in Mykonos Town.

6.Samaria Gorge

Greece, notably the island of Crete, is home to the amazing natural feature known as the Samaria Gorge. The Samaria Gorge has a number of interesting facts, as well as well-known highlights and reasons why it's worthwhile to visit.

- The Samaria Gorge is one of the longest canyons in Europe, measuring over 16 kilometers (10 miles) in length. It is located in Crete's southwest, near the White Mountains (Lefka Ori).

- Samaria National Park, also known as the Samaria Gorge National Park, was established in 1962.

- Approximately 48 square kilometers (19 square miles) in size, the park is home to a variety of plants and animals.

- Scenic Beauty: With its high cliffs, rough terrain, and thick vegetation, the gorge offers spectacular natural beauty.

- The "Iron Gates," a tiny corridor with sheer rock walls as high as 300 meters (984 feet), is one of the breathtaking vistas that visitors can explore.

- The Samaria Gorge is a well-known trekking location that draws outdoor enthusiasts and nature lovers.

- The trail descends through the valley to the settlement of Agia Roumeli on the Libyan Sea coast from the trailhead at Xyloskalo, which is 1,230 meters (4,035 ft) above sea level.

- A diversity of plant species, including rare Cretan endemics like the Cretan ebony (ebenus cretica) and the wild Cretan tulip, can be found in the gorge (tulipa saxatilis).

- The Cretan wild goat (kri-kri), different bird species, and reptiles are among the local wildlife.

- The Samaria Gorge has historical and cultural value because there are still ruins of ancient towns and churches there.

- Within the national park, the deserted settlement of Samaria, after which the gorge is called, provides a window into the past.

- The Samaria National Park is committed to preserving and safeguarding its distinctive environment.

- While enjoying the pure natural settings, visitors can learn about and support conservation activities.

- Tourist Attractions: Traveling down the Samaria Gorge offers an exciting and satisfying trip that enables guests to fully appreciate nature's beauty. The breathtaking scenery, the strenuous but energizing hike, the chance to see rare plants and animals, and the opportunity to see historical places are just a few of the highlights.

- Accessibility & Season: From May through October, when the park is open to the public, visitors can enter the Samaria Gorge.

- To avoid intense heat and crowded areas, spring or autumn are the best times to visit.

- Practical Points: Hiking the Samaria Gorge calls for good physical condition as well as the appropriate hiking supplies, such as strong boots and sun protection.

- It's crucial to be ready and take the proper precautions because the trail can be difficult and has high, uneven terrain.

- The Samaria Gorge in Greece is a must-see location for nature lovers and people looking for a distinctive way to enjoy the breathtaking scenery of Crete. It offers a memorable experience of natural beauty, cultural history, and outdoor adventure.

7.Corfu Town

The capital and main city of the Greek island of Corfu is Corfu Town, often called Kerkyra. Here are some details about Corfu Town and the explanations for why it is a well-liked vacation spot:

- Historical Importance: Corfu Town has a long, illustrious past that goes back to prehistoric times. Greek, Roman, Byzantine, Venetian, and British civilizations, among others, have had an impact on the city. Its historical landmarks and architectural design showcase this rich past.

- The Old Town of Corfu, which includes Corfu Town, was named a UNESCO World Heritage Site in 2007. The Old Town draws tourists from all over the world with its Venetian-style buildings, winding lanes, and attractive squares.

- The Old Fortress and the New Fortress, two outstanding Venetian fortresses, are located in Corfu Town. The Old Fortress, perched atop a rocky outcropping, provides sweeping views of both the city and the ocean. On a hilltop above the village, The New Fortress offers a view into the island's former defensive history.

- Liston Promenade: The Liston is a stunning promenade in Corfu Town that was modeled after Paris's Rue de Rivoli. With cafes, restaurants, and shops, it has magnificent arched buildings. Locals and visitors alike frequently unwind, enjoy a cup of coffee, and take in the lively environment at The Liston.

- Spianada Square is situated close to the Liston and is the biggest square in the Balkans. Cricket matches, concerts, and other cultural events are held in the square, which is a centre of activity. It's a terrific spot to people-watch and take in Corfu Town's buzzing vibe.

- Corfu Town is home to a number of museums and cultural attractions that are well worth visiting. Artifacts from ancient Corfu are on display in the

Archaeological Museum of Corfu, while a sizable collection of works by artists from China, Japan, and India are on view in the Museum of Asian Art. Another must-see site is the Church of Saint Spyridon, which is devoted to Corfu's patron saint.

- Corfu Town has a variety of dining establishments as well as local and foreign retailers. There are numerous stores selling apparel, jewelry, souvenirs, and other items along the city's main shopping streets, such as Kapodistriou and Nikiforou Theotoki. Additionally, Corfu Town is also known for its fantastic dining options, with a wide variety of eateries serving both traditional Greek and other cuisines.

- Corfu Town comes alive after dark and offers a thriving nightlife scene. Everyone may find something to enjoy, from quaint bars and classic taverns to chic clubs and live music places. Streets like Liston and Old Town are especially well-liked for evening strolls and sipping a few drinks.

- Corfu Town doesn't have any sandy beaches, although it is ideally adjacent to some of the island's breathtaking coastline. Beautiful beaches like Glyfada, Paleokastritsa, and Agios Gordios can be easily reached by car or bus for visitors who are willing to travel a little distance.

- Corfu International Airport is located in Corfu Town, making it simple for travelers from around the world to reach the island. It serves as a starting point for exploring the remainder of the island because to its handy location and good transit connections.

Corfu Town, with its blend of history, culture, stunning architecture, and lively atmosphere, offers a delightful experience for visitors, making it a must-visit destination in Greece.

8.Zagorohoria and the Ancient Ruins of Kassope and Nikopolis.

Northwest Greece's Pindus Mountains contain the hilly region of Zagori, commonly referred to as Zagorohoria. It is a breathtaking location renowned for its unspoiled landscapes, historic towns, and outdoor pursuits. The ancient ruins of Kassope and Nikopolis, which provide a look into Greece's rich historical past, are two of the key attractions in the Zagori region. Here are some details and important information about Zagorohoria and these historic ruins:

- 46 traditional villages make up Zagorohoria, a region tucked away in the Zagori mountain range. Beautiful natural scenery, stone-built homes, stone arches, and cobblestone pathways define the area. For those who enjoy the outdoors, hiking, and adventure, it is a well-liked vacation.

- Kassope's Ancient Ruins: The ancient city of Kassope is situated in the Zagorohoria region of Epirus. It offers impressive archaeological remains and was established in the 4th century BC. The theater, agora (marketplace), temples, and defensive walls may all be explored by tourists. The property offers spectacular panoramic vistas.

- Ancient Ruins of Nikopolis: In the Zagorohoria region, close to Preveza, Nikopolis—which means "Victory City"—is a noteworthy archaeological site. At order to remember his triumph over Mark Antony and Cleopatra in the Battle of Actium, the Roman Emperor Augustus constructed it in 31 BC. A theater, stadium, odeon, Roman baths, and the majestic Octagon Monument are among the remnants.

- Historical Importance: Kassope and Nikopolis are both very important historical sites. In ancient Greece, Kassope was a significant city-state that had a significant impact on both trade and politics in the area. On the other hand, Nikopolis was a vibrant Roman metropolis and a significant cultural hub at the period.

- In addition to their historical significance, the sites of these ancient remains are breathtakingly gorgeous. Kassope, which offers amazing views of the surrounding area, is perched on a hill overlooking a valley. Nikopolis is close to the Ambracian Gulf and offers beautiful views of the surrounding landscape and the ocean.

- Outdoor Activities: There are many chances for outdoor activities in Zagorohoria and the surrounding areas of Kassope and Nikopolis. Visitors can engage in outdoor activities like rafting and kayaking on the Voidomatis

River, hike, climb, and mountaineer in the Pindus Mountains, and visit the neighboring Vikos Gorge, one of the deepest gorges in the world.

- Local Customs and Hospitality: Zagorohoria is well known for its friendly people and manner of life. By staying in conventional guesthouses, sampling regional cuisine, and taking part in cultural activities and festivals, tourists can get a taste of the local way of life.

Visiting Zagorohoria and exploring the ancient ruins of Kassope and Nikopolis offers a unique combination of natural beauty, historical significance, and outdoor adventure. It provides a memorable experience for tourists interested in Greece's ancient history and picturesque landscapes.

9.Nafplio

Beautiful Nafplio is a town in Greece's Peloponnese region. It has significant historical value and a pleasant ambience that draws tourists from all over the world. Here are some details about Nafplio and its top attractions to help you decide if you should go there:

- Historical Significance: Following Greece's independence from the Ottoman Empire in 1828, Nafplio served as the nation's first capital. The town has a long history, and the architecture and culture reflect a rich fusion of Venetian, Byzantine, and Ottoman influences.
- The Palamidi Fortress, which is built on a hill above the town of Nafplio, is one of the city's most recognizable

features. It provides amazing views of the surroundings and was constructed by the Venetians in the 18th century. The fortress's 999 steps can be climbed by visitors who then have access to its well-preserved bastions, tunnels, and cells.

- The Bourtzi Fortification, which is situated on a little islet in the midst of Nafplio's bay, is another fortress that is well visiting. It was constructed by the Venetians in the fifteenth century as a fortress to guard the town. Bourtzi is now a well-liked tourist destination that can be reached by boat.

- Old Town: The Old Town of Nafplio is a lovely tangle of winding streets, neoclassical structures, and quaint squares. Visitors can unwind and take in the ambiance in one of the cafes or restaurants lining Syntagma Square, the city's largest square. The town's cobblestone lanes are lined with hidden treasures including quaint stores, art galleries, and age-old taverns.

- The oldest section of Nafplio is called Acronauplia, and it has old towers, gates, and walls. Exploring this location provides a window into the town's early history. Visitors can take in expansive views of the city, the sea, and the neighboring mountains from Acronauplia.

- Museums: Nafplio is the location of a number of fascinating museums. A variety of local antiquities dating back thousands of years are kept in the

Archaeological Museum of Nafplio. In contrast to the Peloponnesian Folklore Foundation Museum, which displays traditional Greek clothing and textiles, the War Museum explores Greece's military history.

- Beaches: The area around Nafplio is endowed with some stunning beaches. With its pristine seas and golden sand, Karathona Beach, just a few kilometers from the town, is a well-liked option. Another beautiful beach, Tolo Beach, is nearby and is well-known for its lengthy sandy beachfront.

- Events and Festivals: Throughout the year, Nafplio is home to a number of festivals and cultural gatherings. The Nafplio Festival takes place in the summer and features performances of music, theater, and dance at distinctive locations all across the city. The Armata Festival, which takes place in September, honors a famous naval conflict and features a festive celebration with fireworks and a live performance.

10. Medieval Town of Rhodes

One of the best-preserved medieval towns in Europe is the Medieval Town of Rhodes, which is situated on the Greek island of Rhodes. It is a UNESCO World Heritage Site. The following information about the town, its tourist attractions, and reasons to go there:

- Historical Importance: The Knights Hospitaller founded the medieval town of Rhodes in the 14th century, and it served as their headquarters of operations while fighting in the Crusades. It was a key location in the history of the Eastern Mediterranean and was home to many different civilizations and cultures over the years.

- Impressive Fortifications: The Knights Hospitaller built the massive medieval walls that surround the town, which are regarded as among of the best examples of fortifications from that time period. There are seven gates along the roughly 4-kilometer-long walls, and each gate has a distinct personality.

- Palace of the Grand Master: The Palace of the Grand Master is one of the town's most notable landmarks. It was initially constructed in the 14th century and used to house the Grand Master of the Knights Hospitaller. It now serves as a museum with a view of the town and a collection of medieval antiques.

- Street of the Knights: The inns of the many knightly orders, including the Knights of Saint John, who originally resided in Rhodes, line this charming cobblestone street. The Street of the Knights' setting and architecture transport visitors back to the Middle Ages.

- The Rhodes Archaeological Museum is housed within the city's medieval walls and features a sizable collection of ancient Rhodes artifacts, including pottery, jewelry, and sculptures. It is a fantastic location to learn about the history of the island and the various civilizations that have called it home.

- Gothic Architecture: Magnificent specimens of Gothic architecture may be seen in the Medieval Town of Rhodes. These structures are distinguished by their exquisite stonework, vaulted ceilings, and ornate façade. Visitors can see the intricate craftsmanship of the medieval era while strolling through the winding streets.

- Beautiful Byzantine churches may be found all across the town, highlighting the Byzantine Empire's impact on the island. Examples of churches with beautiful frescoes and religious icons include the Church of Panagia tou Kastrou and the Church of Agios Fanourios.

- Attractive Atmosphere: The town's winding lanes, which are surrounded with vibrant structures, cute stores, and charming cafes, produce a special and romantic atmosphere. Indulge in regional food, take leisurely strolls, and take in the lively ambiance of this thriving medieval town.

- Acropolis of Rhodes: The Acropolis of Rhodes, which belongs to the Hellenistic era, is located just outside the medieval fortifications. You can visit historic ruins, including a stadium and a temple, and it provides panoramic views of the town and its surroundings.

- Mediterranean Climate: The Medieval Town is located on Rhodes Island, which has a Mediterranean climate with moderate winters and scorching summers. This makes it a great place to visit if you want good weather, gorgeous beaches, and a mix of historical and natural attractions.

The Medieval Town of Rhodes is a captivating destination that seamlessly blends history, culture, and beauty. With its well-preserved medieval architecture, intriguing museums, and a vibrant atmosphere, it offers a unique travel experience for history enthusiasts and those seeking a journey back in time.

Famous Greek Architectural Wonders

The Parthenon Temple

One of Greece's most recognizable structures and a UNESCO World Heritage site is the Parthenon Temple. It is an architectural marvel and a representation of ancient Greek culture that may be found on the Acropolis hill in Athens. The Parthenon is described in depth here, along with tourist attractions, fees, regulations, and other pertinent information.:

1. Architecture and History:

   - The renowned sculptor Phidias oversaw the construction of the Parthenon between 447 and 432 BCE, during the Golden Age of Athens.

   - It was built as a temple for the goddess Athena Parthenos, who was revered as Athens' patron saint.

- The architects Ictinus and Callicrates were in charge of the temple's design, and Phidias was in charge of the decorative artwork and sculptures.

- A Doric temple made entirely of marble, the Parthenon is admired for its outstanding symmetry, pleasing proportions, and exquisite workmanship.

2. Tourist Highlights:

   - From its vantage point atop the Acropolis, the Parthenon provides stunning views of Athens and its surroundings.

   - Ancient Greek craftsmanship is evident in the temple's architectural details, which include the fluted columns, pediments, friezes, and metopes.

   - The Parthenon's west pediment represents the struggle between Athena and Poseidon for control of Athens, while the east pediment shows the birth of Athena.

   - A massive statue of Athena created by Phidias and kept at the Parthenon was composed of gold and ivory. Sadly, the statue has vanished.

3. Charges and Opening Hours:

   - Adults must pay €20 for general entrance to the Acropolis, which grants them access to the Parthenon.

- Senior citizens and students both receive discounted prices. Under-18s are admitted free of charge.

- Please be aware that these fees could vary, so it's best to check the official websites or get in touch with the authorities for the most recent details.

- Depending on the season, the hours of operation change. The Parthenon typically remains open from 8:00 AM until 8:00 PM in the summer and until 5:00 PM in the winter.

4. Rules and Regulations:

- While visiting the Parthenon, various guidelines and standards must be adhered to in order to protect the historical site.

- No objects or architectural components may be touched or taken away by visitors.

- Tripods, selfie sticks, and other tools that could harm the property are not permitted.

- Vandalism of any kind, including sitting on the columns or climbing the old buildings, is absolutely forbidden.

- For their safety and the preservation of the area, visitors are urged to respect the signs, barriers, and designated walkways.

Erechthion

On Athens' Acropolis, near the Parthenon, stands the ancient Greek temple known as the Erechtheion. It is a recognizable and impressively designed structure that draws lots of tourists every year. Here are some specifics on the Erechtheion.

1. Architecture and Highlights:

    -   During the Golden Age of Athens, which lasted from 421 to 406 BCE, the Erechtheion was constructed. It was created by Mnesicles, a renowned architect.

    -   Both Athena Polias and Poseidon-Erechtheus, two significant deities in ancient Greek mythology, are honored in this temple.

    -   The Erechtheion's porch, sometimes referred to as the Caryatid Porch or Porch of the Maidens, is its most recognizable feature. It is supported by six marble columns that are sculpted with feminine figurines called caryatids.

    -   The frieze that extends along the temple's exterior walls and features scenes from Greek mythology and history is another noteworthy aspect.

    -   The architecture of the temple combines several architectural forms, notably the Ionic order and the Erechtheion's own peculiar design, to create a singular structure.

- Visitors are welcome to explore the east chamber, west chamber, and north porch, among other chambers and sanctuaries, inside the Erechtheion.

2. Charges and Opening Hours:

- The Erechtheion and other Acropolis monuments are accessible with the general admission Acropolis ticket. Adult tickets cost about €20, while reduced-price tickets cost about €10. (e.g., students, seniors).

- It's important to keep in mind, though, that rules and ticket prices are subject to change, so it's best to check the official website or get in touch with the local authorities for the most recent details.

3. Rules and Regulations:

- Certain laws and restrictions are normally upheld in order to guarantee the site's preservation and improve visitor safety. These might include limits on touching the historic buildings, smoking bans, and rules against using tripods or flash photography.

- Visitors are urged to stay on authorized trails and to avoid straying into off-limits territory.

- Furthermore, it's critical to respect the site's historical and cultural significance by refraining from littering and inflicting any harm to the buildings.

4. Visitor Tips:

- To avoid crowds and the warmest part of the day during the summer, it is advised to visit the Erechtheion and the Acropolis early in the day or later in the afternoon.

- Since there are stairs and uneven ground, it is best to wear comfortable shoes.

- It is imperative to bring sunscreen, a hat, and drink because the site may be exposed to the sun, especially during the summer.

Temple of Apollo

An old Doric temple in Greece called the Temple of Apollo is devoted to the Apollon divinity. I don't have access to current information or specifics regarding recent updates, but I can give you a general overview of the temple based on what I know about it historically as of September 2021. Before making travel arrangements, it's always a good idea to confirm the most recent information from dependable sources or tourism websites.

Location: The Temple of Apollo, also called the Temple of Delphi, is found in Delphi, a small settlement in central Greece that is perched on the slopes of Mount Parnassus. In the past, Delphi was revered as the center of the globe and was known for its oracle, where people sought the predictions of Apollo.

Tourist Highlights:

- Known for its magnificent Doric architectural style, the Temple of Apollo is a beautifully preserved ancient Greek temple. It has strong limestone columns, a colonnaded facade, and a frieze that depicts numerous mythical episodes. It was built around the 4th century BCE.

- Delphi's extensive archaeological complex also includes the Sanctuary of Athena Pronaia, the Tholos of Delphi, the ancient theater, and the Stadium. This is in addition to the Temple of Apollo. Visitors can get a taste of the theological and cultural significance of ancient Delphi by exploring these ruins.

- The famed Charioteer of Delphi, a bronze figure of a charioteer, is housed in the Delphi Museum, which is close to the archaeological site. Other notable items in the museum's collection include votive offerings and statues that were unearthed during excavations.

Charges and Rules: Please be aware that charges and rules are subject to change at any time, therefore it is important to check with official sources for the most current and correct information. Here are some general principles:

- Entry fees: The archaeological site and the museum typically charge admission. Adults, students, and older citizens may pay different costs. There may occasionally be multi-attraction combination tickets available for the Delphi complex.

- Opening Times: The site and museum normally have set hours of operation, which may change according to the time of year. It's a good idea to check the opening times in advance so you can schedule your visit appropriately.

- Photography and videography: There may be laws governing photography and filming. While shooting photos for personal use is frequently permitted, there can be limitations if the photos are being taken for work or for a business. Tripods or other apparatus might need a special permit.

- Respectful Behaviour: It's crucial to respect the historical significance of the site when visiting the Temple of Apollo and the neighborhood. Avoid destroying or removing any artifacts by paying attention to any instructions or signage that may be there.

Great Theatre of Epidaurus

A prominent ancient theater called the Great Theatre of Epidaurus can be found in the Greek archaeological site of the same name. It is regarded as one of the most remarkable and well-preserved antique theaters in the entire world. The Great Theatre of Epidaurus is described in depth here, along with its tourist attractions, fees, policies, and other pertinent information:

1. Background information: The architect Polykleitos the Younger is credited with designing the Great Theatre of Epidaurus, which was constructed in the fourth century

BCE. It was a portion of the Asklepios Sanctuary, a hospital honoring the Greek deity of medicine.

2. Architecture and acoustics: The theater is round and has a seating capacity of about 14,000 people. Because of its outstanding acoustics, even a stage whisper may be heard across the entire theater. The theater's layout enables optimum sound amplification without the use of any electrical equipment.

3. Performances: During the Epidaurus Festival, which takes place every year from July through August, the theater is largely used to hold ancient Greek drama performances. The festival draws theater lovers from all around the world and presents a range of classic plays. It's crucial to remember that the theater occasionally hosts other cultural activities in addition to these shows.

4. Prices and Business Hours: Adult admission to the Great Theatre of Epidaurus costs roughly 12 euros. The location normally opens early in the morning and closes in the late afternoon, though the hours can change depending on the season. For the most recent details on costs and hours of operation, it is advised to consult the official website or get in touch with the local authorities.

5. Rules & Regulations: The following guidelines should be followed when visiting the Great Theatre of Epidaurus:

   • It is not permitted to touch or climb the historic buildings.

- The steps leading up to the theater can be steep and uneven, therefore visitors are urged to wear appropriate footwear.

- The use of tripods or professional filming equipment may need a specific permit, however taking pictures for personal use is typically permitted.

- Inside the theater, visitors are required to keep a courteous and calm demeanor.

6. Other Attractions in the Area: In addition to the Sanctuary of Asklepios, the ancient site of Epidaurus also has the Tholos of Epidaurus, a circular structure, and the Epidaurus Museum. These landmarks offer additional insights into the region's ancient history and culture.

Knossos Palace

One of the most significant and well-known historical sites in the nation is the ancient archaeological site of Knossos Palace, which is situated on the Greek island of Crete. The following provides comprehensive information about Knossos Palace, including its tourist attractions, fees, policies, and other pertinent information:

1. Overview: Knossos Palace is an ancient Minoan palace complex that dates back to the Bronze Age. It was the ceremonial and political center of the Minoan civilization, which flourished around 2000 to 1450 BCE. The palace was first constructed around 1900 BCE

and was continuously expanded and rebuilt over the centuries.

2. Tourist Highlights:

- Grand Staircase: The Grand Staircase, which leads to the central courtyard, is one of the palace's most spectacular features. It is decorated with vibrant frescoes that show a variety of Minoan life events.

- Throne Room: The Throne Room is thought to have served as the palace's ceremonial and power center. It has colorful frescoes and a rebuilt throne.

- The Queen's Megaron contains well-preserved frescoes of the "Ladies in Blue" and the "Dolphin Fresco," which are assumed to have been the queen's private chambers.

- Royal Road: The Little Palace, which is thought to be a residential neighborhood, is connected to the palace by the Royal Road. Visitors can get a sense of the palace's layout and magnificence by strolling down this path.

- Storage Magazines: The palace contained large "magazines" for storing goods, including wheat, olive oil, and other supplies. You can explore a few of these storage spaces.

3. Charges and Opening Hours:

- Knossos Palace charges an entrance price of 16 euros for adults and 8 euros for discounted admission (students, senior citizens, etc.).

- Please be aware that prices and hours may change, so it's best to check the official website or contact the location for the most recent information.

4. Rules and Regulations:

- Non-commercial photography is typically permitted on the property. Tripods and flash photography, however, could be forbidden or limited in some places.

- Visitors are expected to treat the historical site and its objects with respect. In order to protect the delicate artifacts, it is normally forbidden to touch the frescoes or walls.

- Guided Tours: At Knossos Palace, guided tours are offered. Joining one can help you better appreciate the site's significance and history.

- Facilities for visitors: The location has amenities like restrooms, a small cafe, and a gift shop.

Temple of Hephaestus

The Hephaisteion or Theseion, commonly known as the Temple of Hephaestus, is an ancient Greek temple that may be seen in Athens, Greece, on the western slope of the Acropolis. It is a noteworthy archaeological site and one of the best-preserved Doric temples in the nation. The Temple of Hephaestus is described in depth below, along with tourist attractions, fees, regulations, and other crucial information:

1. History and Architecture:

- In the fifth century BCE, between 449 and 415 BCE, during Pericles' Golden Age, the Temple of Hephaestus was constructed.

- It was dedicated to Hephaestus, the Greek god of fire, metalworking, and workmanship.

- Ictinus, the architect who is also credited with creating the Parthenon, was the designer of the temple.

- The temple's Doric architecture is recognizable by its solid, manly aspect and its straightforward, rectangular floor plan.

- It has a pronaos (porch), a cella (inner chamber), and an opisthodomos and is composed of Pentelic marble (rear chamber).

2. Tourist Highlights:

- Visitors can view a magnificent specimen of classical Greek architecture at the well-preserved historical site known as the Temple of Hephaestus.

- Panoramic views of Athens are available from the temple, including those of the neighboring Acropolis and the surrounding area.

- The remains of the old altar, which was used to offer sacrifices to Hephaestus, may be seen inside the temple.

- Greek mythological events, such as Hercules' labors and the conflict between Theseus and the Centaurs, are depicted on the friezes of the temple.

3. Charges and Opening Hours:

   - The combined ticket for the Athens archaeological sites, which costs €20 for adults and is good for five days, includes access to the Temple of Hephaestus. It's always a good idea to double-check for updates or adjustments to entrance prices, though.

   - Opening times fluctuate throughout the year, but are normally from dawn till dusk. Prior to your visit, it is essential to establish the precise opening times as they may change owing to seasonal changes or unanticipated events.

4. Rules and Etiquette:

   - In order to protect the Temple of Hephaestus for future generations, visitors must abide by the laws and regulations established by the archaeological authorities.

   - No parts of the temple's architecture or artifacts may be handled or taken out.

   - Observe the warnings and obstacles put in place to safeguard the temple's building.

- In general, photography is permitted, however using tripods or additional lighting can need special authorization.

- As the area around the temple might be uneven, it is advised to dress modestly and wear comfortable shoes.

Temple of Artemis

The magnificent ancient Greek temple known as the Temple of Artemis, sometimes called the Artemision, was devoted to the goddess Artemis. It was situated at Ephesus, a city that is currently a part of Turkey but was once a part of Greece. The temple, which was known for its majesty and beauty, was one of the Seven Wonders of the Ancient World. Even if the temple is no longer standing, I can give you comprehensive information about its historical importance, tourist attractions, fees (if any), laws, and other pertinent specifics.

1. Historical Significance:

    - One of the most significant religious structures in the ancient Greek world, the Temple of Artemis was constructed in the sixth century BCE.

    - The well-known Greek architect Chersiphron and his son Metagenes were responsible for its creation.

- The Greek goddess Artemis, who is associated with the hunt, wildlife, and fertility, among other things, was honored in the temple.

- It was thought to be a location for devotion and pilgrimage, drawing followers from a great distance.

2. Tourist Highlights:

- Even though the temple is now in ruins, exploring the Ephesus archaeological site offers the chance to discover the remains of this historic marvel.

- The location has the foundation, columns, and sculptures of the temple still standing, providing a glimpse into its previous opulence.

- The adjacent Ephesus Museum and the British Museum in London both house some of the remaining sculptures and relics from the temple.

- Guided tours of Ephesus frequently include a stop at the Temple of Artemis, allowing tourists to see the Great Theater and other magnificent ancient buildings nearby.

3. Charges:

- There are no special fees for visiting the site of the Temple of Artemis because the temple itself is no longer there.

- The area where the temple originally stood is part of Ephesus' wider archaeological site, which may require payment of an entrance fee. Depending on the particular rules and procedures in effect at the time of your visit, the fees may change.

- For the most recent information on entrance fees and other costs, it is advised to contact local tourism bureaus or visit the Ephesus archaeological site's official website.

4. Rules and Guidelines:

- To protect the historical integrity of Ephesus' archaeological site, visitors must adhere to the regulations put forth by the site's administrators.

- Usually, visitors are asked to show respect for the location by not damaging the remains in any way, including by littering or defacing them.

- It is highly forbidden to climb the historic buildings or remove objects from the location.

- For safety concerns, visitors are urged to stay on authorized walkways and to stay out of restricted areas.

- Photography and filming may be permitted for personal use depending on the site and local laws, however using tripods and other professional equipment would need a specific permit.

The Temple of Zeus

The Olympieion, commonly referred to as the Columns of the Olympian Zeus or the Temple of Zeus, is a historic temple that can be seen in Athens, Greece. One of the biggest temples in the nation, it is also a significant archaeological site. Here are some specifics on the Temple of Zeus:

Location: The Temple of Zeus is situated southeast of the Acropolis, in the heart of Athens. It is located within the archaeological site of the ancient city.

Historical Significance: Construction of the temple began in the 6th century BCE but was not completed until the reign of the Roman Emperor Hadrian in the 2nd century CE. It was dedicated to Zeus, the king of the Greek gods and the ruler of Mount Olympus. The temple was a magnificent structure, showcasing the power and grandeur of the gods.

Tourist Highlights: The Temple of Zeus offers visitors a glimpse into ancient Greek architecture and mythology. Although only a few columns remain standing today, they are still awe-inspiring. The temple originally had 104 columns, each reaching a height of approximately 17 meters (56 feet). The sheer scale of the temple is a testament to the ancient Greeks' engineering skills.

Close to the temple, visitors can see the Arch of Hadrian, an imposing marble gateway erected by Emperor Hadrian. It served as a symbolic entrance to the city of Athens.

Charges and Rules: To visit the Temple of Zeus, you need to purchase a ticket for the archaeological site, which includes access to several other ancient landmarks in Athens. the ticket price for the combined archaeological site, including the Acropolis, is around 20 euros for adults. However, please note that ticket prices and rules may change, so it's best to check with the official authorities or tourist information centers for up-to-date information.

When visiting the temple or any other archaeological site, it's important to follow certain rules and guidelines to preserve these historical treasures. Some general rules include:

1. Respect the site: Treat the temple and its surroundings with respect. Do not climb on the ancient structures or touch the ancient stones.

2. No littering: Keep the area clean and dispose of any trash in designated bins.

3. Photography: Feel free to take photographs for personal use, but be mindful not to use flash photography if it's prohibited, as it can cause damage to ancient artifacts.

4. Stay on designated paths: Follow the designated paths and avoid stepping on restricted areas.

It's advisable to check with the official authorities or signage at the site for any specific rules or restrictions that may be in place during your visit.

The Temple of Zeus is a remarkable archaeological site that offers visitors a chance to witness the grandeur of ancient

Greek architecture and mythology. Exploring this site can be a captivating experience for history enthusiasts and tourists alike

The Temple of Hera

The Heraion, sometimes referred to as the Temple of Hera, is a historic Greek temple that may be found in Olympia, Greece. The goddess Hera, the mother of the Greek gods and the wife of Zeus, is honored by its dedication. The temple, one of Greece's most important archaeological sites, draws lots of visitors each year. Here are some specifics on the Temple of Hera:

Location: The Temple of Hera is situated within the archaeological site of Olympia, in the western part of the Peloponnese region in Greece. Olympia was the birthplace of the Olympic Games and holds great historical and cultural importance.

Historical Significance: The temple was constructed around the 7th century BCE and underwent several expansions and renovations over the centuries. It was part of the larger sanctuary of Olympia, which included various religious and athletic structures. The Temple of Hera served as a religious center and was used for the worship of Hera during the Olympic Games.

Architectural Features: The Temple of Hera is built in the Doric architectural style, characterized by its simple and sturdy design. It is peripteral, meaning it is surrounded by a single row of columns on all sides. The temple originally had six columns on the front and back, and sixteen columns on the sides. Today, only the remains of these columns and parts of the entablature are visible.

Tourist Highlights: Visiting the Temple of Hera provides an opportunity to explore the ancient ruins and immerse oneself in Greek history. Some highlights include:

- Temple Ruins: Explore the remains of the temple and marvel at the surviving columns and architectural elements that give a glimpse into its past glory.

- Altar of Hera: Located in front of the temple, the altar was used for making offerings and sacrifices during religious ceremonies.

- Archaeological Museum: Within the Olympia site, there is an archaeological museum that houses a collection of artifacts found in the area, including sculptures, statues, and relics from the ancient Olympic Games.

Charges and Rules: To visit the Temple of Hera and the Olympia archaeological site, there is an entrance fee. The exact charges may vary, so it's advisable to check the official website or local tourist information for up-to-date prices. As for rules, visitors are typically expected to adhere to the following guidelines:

- Respect the Site: Treat the ruins with respect and avoid touching or causing damage to the ancient structures.

- No Littering: Keep the site clean by disposing of any trash in designated bins.

- Follow Instructions: Follow any instructions or signs provided by the authorities or guides.

- Photography: Photography is usually allowed, but the use of tripods or professional equipment may require permission or an additional fee.

- Dress Code: While there might not be strict dress codes, it is recommended to dress modestly and comfortably, taking into consideration the cultural and historical significance of the site.

Visiting the Temple of Hera in Greece offers a fascinating insight into ancient Greek civilization, architecture, and mythology. It is a must-visit destination for history enthusiasts and anyone interested in experiencing the rich cultural heritage of Greece.

Odeon of Herodes Atticus

The Herodion, often referred to as the Odeon of Herodes Atticus, is a historic amphitheater that is situated on the southwest side of the Acropolis in Athens, Greece. One of the oldest theaters in the world that has been preserved the best is this one. The Odeon of Herodes Atticus is described in detail below, along with tourist attractions, fees, regulations, and other pertinent information:

1. History and Architecture:

    - The Odeon of Herodes Atticus was built in 161 AD by the Athenian magnate Herodes Atticus in memory of his wife.

- The theater was primarily used for musical performances and could accommodate up to 5,000 spectators.

- The structure was originally roofed, but it was destroyed in the 3rd century AD and never rebuilt.

- Today, the Odeon is renowned for its exceptional acoustics and stunning architecture.

2. Tourist Highlights:

- The Odeon of Herodes Atticus is an iconic landmark and a popular tourist attraction in Athens.

- Visitors can marvel at the ancient theater's grand structure, made of Pentelic marble.

- The stage wall and the rows of stone seats are still intact, providing a glimpse into the theater's ancient glory.

- The theater is occasionally used for live performances, including ancient Greek plays, concerts, and cultural events, especially during the Athens & Epidaurus Festival in the summer.

3. Charges and Access:

- Access to the Odeon of Herodes Atticus is included in the combined ticket for the archaeological sites of Athens, which costs €30

- The combined ticket grants entry to several other archaeological sites, including the Acropolis, the Ancient Agora, the Roman Agora, and more.

- The ticket is valid for five days and can be purchased at any of the participating sites.

- It's advisable to check the official website or local tourist information for the most up-to-date information on ticket prices and access.

4. Rules and Regulations:

- To ensure the preservation of the ancient theater, there are certain rules and regulations that visitors must follow.

- Climbing on the seats or any part of the structure is strictly prohibited.

- Visitors are expected to respect the historical significance of the site and refrain from any actions that may damage the theater.

- Photography is allowed, but the use of tripods and professional equipment may require special permission.

- During live performances, specific rules and etiquette may apply, such as no photography or video recording.

5. Nearby Attractions:

- While visiting the Odeon of Herodes Atticus, you can explore other nearby attractions, including the Acropolis, the Parthenon, the Theatre of Dionysus, and the Acropolis Museum.

- These sites offer a deeper insight into ancient Greek history, art, and culture.

Best Beaches in Greece

Greece is well-known throughout the world for its stunning beaches. This nation is renowned for its emerald-green waters and white sandy beaches, which provide a stunning contrast and render the nation picture-perfect. Greece has several beaches, mostly distributed over the mainland but also in some of the best Greek islands of the Aegean and Ionian Sea, where you can see some of the best vistas. You will have an amazing trip experience thanks to the inviting, sun-kissed coolness of the crystal-clear water.

Lalaria

The only way to get to the remote and stunning Lalaria Beach is via boat from Skiathos town. Lalaria is an idyllic place with its white sand beaches and breathtaking cliffs rising from the sea. You'll have trouble putting this amazing beach's enchantment into words. It is the emblem of the island, frequently named the most beautiful beach, and is well-known throughout the globe. Numerous people are drawn to the white stones and emerald sea beneath the imposing vertical rocks every day. When the boats arrive, you can spend your time swimming on a pristine, undeveloped beach on the Sporades islands, with only the wild goats grazing on the hill above as your sole company.

Voidokoilia

You may marvel how this picture-perfect beach with its white sand and emerald-green sea managed to form a perfect semicircle. Homer also makes reference to this ideal form of Voidokoilia in The Odyssey. Spend some time exploring the neighborhood and lazing on the golden sand beach. It won't take long, and you'll feel completely at ease. A fortification from the thirteenth century that was constructed on the remains of classical Pylos is located to the south of the shore. Since this region is regarded as a nudist area, the sound end of the beach may appeal to the local naturalists. People who enjoy letting everything hang loose are drawn to this area of the beach.

Canal d'Amour.

One of the most popular beaches in Greece is Canal d'Amour. Young couples that come to enjoy the stunning sunset vista are the main target audience. The lunar rock formations, which are situated between the Sidari and Peroulades, produce three small waterways that resemble canals. The peculiar feature known as Canal d'Amour stands out. They claim that whomever makes it through the little crack in the rock will meet their soul mate waiting for them on the other side. This beach is ideal for snorkeling, swimming, and dicing.

Katsiki Porto

One of the top six beaches in the entire Mediterranean may be found at Lefkas, at the base of a huge, white cliff that glows orange at sunset. Compared to other beaches in Greece, it boasts the most stunning scenery. Relax on one of Greece's most famous beaches as you take in the magnificence of the ocean and its azure blue waters. You can lounge along the relatively short stretch of sand here while renting an umbrella. The best time to visit Porto Katsiki, one of the most popular tourist attractions, is in the early morning, around 8 am. Despite the fact that it could become crowded as the day goes on, you should still schedule some time to visit.

Sarakiniko

A group of volcanic rock covers make up Sarakiniko Beach. This volcanic rock has been shaped into strange shapes by the wind and the waves, giving you the impression that you are walking on the moon. These milky-white, chalk-soft boulders have been shaped into fascinating forms by the sand and waves. As you get farther from the shore, the deep gulf's green water changes to blue water in all its colors. This beach has personality, which makes it among the best in Greece. It is claimed to have gotten its name from the Saracan pirates who sought refuge here and is situated in the northernmost, windiest region of the Greek island of Milos.

Kolymbithres

This well-known beach is tucked away in the bay of Naoussa and features stunning blue-green water, smooth grayish rocks that have been chiseled into fantastical patterns, and tasty golden coves of various sizes. This Paros beach is a forgotten Greek hero. There are several isolated coves surrounded by stunning granite rock where you may relax with your family. A top-notch beachside restaurant serving the catch of the day just adds to the delight. Numerous secluded coves can be found here that can be explored on foot or by swimming, and a variety of facilities are offered for your comfort.

Elafonisi

The little, unspoiled peninsula of Elafonisi is located west of Chania. This beach is well-known for its vibrant pink sand, calm seas, and dense cedar woodland. It is best to travel there by vehicle or boat for a day trip. It is regarded as the island's cleanest and best-maintained beach. The shimmering, ground-up coral-like material is abundant on Elafonisi. The beach is wonderful and clear, and it is a protected natural reserve. Arrive early to relax and take in the beach's splendor since it becomes more crowded as the day wears on. If you enjoy extreme activities, this is the place to go. Windsurfing is a great sport here. Summertime offers ideal surfing conditions practically every day.

Balos

This beach, which is regarded as one of the best in the Mediterranean, is among the most exotic beaches in all of Greece. Balos is essentially located in western Crete, close to Kissamo. The ocean is a stunning combination of blue and green, and the sand is pink and white. The area is given a fairy-tale feel by the islet of Gramvousa and its Venetian castle. It is claimed to have a mythological Greek origin. This breathtaking location, which is near the Balos Lagoon, is also proud of its own historical significance. Hike through the bird reserve, visit the remnants of a castle from the thirteenth century, or go windsurfing on the bay.

Myrtos

This gorgeous beach is located halfway between Assos and Argostoli. This location will transport you to a new dimension thanks to the white sand and little stones, the turquoise waters, and the base of impossibly high cliffs. If you climb the peninsula to the north, you will see some of the breathtaking vistas from here. With its tall surrounding hills and stunning turquoise waves, this westward facing beach is regarded as one of the best beaches in Greece. It also offers some of the most breathtaking sunset views, making Myrtos' natural beauty unequaled in the entire world. Hike to the perch on the northern headland for views over Hollywood. There is plenty of room for everyone on the long and wide Myrtos beach.

Navagio

Navagio, also known as the Shipwreck Beach, is one of Greece's most famous beaches. This beach has a shipwreck legend from the 1980s, yet despite its challenging accessibility, people still flock to it in the summer. The sharp contrast between the beautiful white sand and the deep blue sea mostly draws them in. One of the most picturesque sights you will ever see is at Navagio Beach. With its towering white cliffs, blue ocean, and white sand, the beach where it ran aground creates a stunning scene. You'll be compelled to jump into its breathtakingly clean water.

Chapter 3: Itineraries

Having an itinerary for your visit to Greece is beneficial for several reasons, as it helps you maximize your time, ensure smooth travel logistics, and make the most of your experience in this diverse and captivating country. Here are some reasons why having an itinerary is essential:

1. Optimizing Your Time: Greece is a country rich in history, culture, and natural beauty, with countless attractions and activities to explore. An itinerary helps you prioritize the places you want to visit and the experiences you want to have, allowing you to make the most of your time and cover as much ground as possible during your stay.

2. Managing Logistics: Greece's geography, consisting of mainland regions and numerous islands, can present logistical challenges when planning transportation, accommodations, and activities. An itinerary helps you organize your travel arrangements in advance, including flights, ferries, accommodation bookings, and transportation between destinations, ensuring a seamless and stress-free travel experience.

3. Avoiding Overcrowding and Disappointment: Popular tourist destinations in Greece, such as Santorini, Mykonos, and Athens, can become crowded, especially during peak travel seasons. By having an itinerary, you can schedule visits to popular attractions during off-peak hours or explore lesser-known gems to avoid

overcrowding and long queues, ensuring a more enjoyable and immersive experience.

4. Exploring Diverse Destinations: Greece offers a diverse range of destinations, each with its own unique charm and attractions. An itinerary allows you to plan visits to multiple regions, including ancient archaeological sites, picturesque islands, charming villages, and vibrant cities, ensuring you get a comprehensive taste of what Greece has to offer.

5. Budgeting and Cost Management: Planning an itinerary enables you to estimate and budget for travel expenses, including accommodation costs, transportation fees, entrance fees to attractions, and dining expenses. By having a clear plan in place, you can make informed decisions about where to allocate your budget and avoid overspending during your trip.

6. Flexibility and Adaptability: While having an itinerary provides structure and organization to your trip, it's essential to maintain flexibility and allow for spontaneity along the way. Your itinerary should be a guide rather than a rigid schedule, allowing you to adapt to unforeseen circumstances, weather changes, or unexpected opportunities that may arise during your travels.

In summary, having an itinerary for your visit to Greece allows you to optimize your time, manage logistics, avoid overcrowding, explore diverse destinations, budget effectively, and maintain flexibility during your travels. Whether you're embarking on a cultural journey through ancient ruins, island-hopping in the Aegean Sea, or indulging in Mediterranean cuisine, a well-planned itinerary enhances your overall travel experience and ensures a memorable adventure in Greece.

one-week itinerary

Athens, Santorini, and Mykonos might all be visited during a weeklong trip to Greece. Here is a recommended route:

Day 1: Arrival in Athens

- Arrive in Greece's capital city of Athens.

- Discover the Acropolis, the Parthenon, and the Ancient Agora, three of Athens' historical sites.

- While dining at a small taverna, stroll through the lovely Plaka area.

Day 2: Athens

- A sizable collection of Greek artifacts can be seen at the National Archaeological Museum.

- Discover the colorful district of Monastiraki, which is renowned for its flea market and energetic ambiance.

- Visit the Panathenaic Stadium, the site of the first modern Olympic Games, or take a stroll around the lovely National Gardens.

Day 3: Santorini

- Visit Santorini, one of Greece's most stunning islands, by ferry or plane.

- Discover the picturesque Oia village with its recognizable blue-domed churches and breathtaking sunset vistas.

- Visit the historic site of Akrotiri, a Minoan town that has been preserved and covered in volcanic ash.

- A sunset sail around the caldera is fun, or you may unwind on one of the island's well-known black sand beaches.

Day 4: Santorini

- Explore the quaint streets of Fira's capital city, which are lined with stores, cafes, and eateries.

- Take a boat journey to Nea Kameni, a volcanic island, then trek to the crater for sweeping views.

- Visit a traditional winery or one of the island's vineyards to sample the regional wines.

Day 5: Mykonos

- From the lively island of Santorini, take a ferry to Mykonos.

- Discover the picturesque alleyways and white-washed structures that make up Mykonos Town's streets.

- Visit the island's recognizable windmills, which serve as its emblem.

- Unwind on one of Mykonos' stunning beaches, such as Paradise Beach or Super Paradise Beach.

Day 6: Mykonos

- Take a boat journey to the nearby island of Delos, which is home to the mythological birthplaces of Apollo and Artemis and is a UNESCO World Heritage site.

- Enjoy Mykonos' vibrant nightlife, which includes its renowned clubs and seaside bars.

- Try some traditional Greek fare at one of the island's tavernas to get a taste of the regional cuisine.

Day 7: Departure

You might have some free time to explore Mykonos before leaving, depending on the time of your departure.

Return to Athens via ferry or plane to complete your departure.

five days itinerary

If you have five days to spend in Greece, you can focus on exploring Athens and one or two nearby islands. Here's a suggested five-day itinerary:

Day 1: Athens

- As soon as you get there, you can begin exploring Athens.

- Visit the well-known Acropolis and have a look at its historic buildings, such as the Parthenon and the Temple of Athena Nike.

- Explore the old Plaka district, which is renowned for its quaint shops, tavernas, and small lanes.

- Discover the center of ancient Athens, the Ancient Agora, where Socrates and Plato once strolled.

Day 2: Athens

- Visit the National Archaeological Museum, which has a sizable collection of items from the ancient Greek world.

- Discover the Monastiraki area, known for its thriving flea market and energetic ambiance.

- Wander through the lovely Anafiotika neighborhood, a little area with a Cycladic island feel that is situated beneath the Acropolis.

Day 3: Day trip to Hydra or Aegina Option 1: Day trip to Hydra

- Take a ferry from Athens to the lovely island of Hydra, which is devoid of automobiles.

- Discover Hydra, a little village renowned for its waterfront views, tiny streets, and preserved architecture.

- Take a leisurely stroll down the beach and stop by the ancient Hydra Museum.

Option 2: Day trip to Aegina

- Take a ferry from Athens to the lovely island of Aegina, which is noted for its ancient ruins and pistachio plantations.

- A Doric temple from the fifth century BC, the Temple of Aphaia is still in good condition.

- Discover the bustling town of Aegina, indulge in regional cuisine, and unwind on the island's beaches.

Day 4: Island Exploration (Santorini or Mykonos) Option 1: Santorini

- From Athens, take a flight or ferry to Santorini, one of the most well-known and stunning Greek islands.

- Discover the quaint village of Oia, famous for its blue-domed churches, whitewashed structures, and breathtaking sunset vistas.

- Visit the historic site of Akrotiri, a Bronze Age Minoan village that has been preserved beneath volcanic ash.

- Enjoy the regional food while unwinding on the island's distinctive black or red sand beaches.

Option 2: Mykonos

- Take a flight or ferry from Athens to Mykonos, a popular island known for its vibrant nightlife and picturesque beaches.

- Explore the charming streets of Mykonos Town, known for its white-washed buildings and iconic windmills.

- Spend the day relaxing on the island's beautiful beaches, such as Paradise Beach or Super Paradise Beach.

- Experience the lively nightlife of Mykonos, with its famous clubs and beachfront bars.

Day 5: Departure

- Depending on your departure time, you may have some free time to explore the island or return to Athens.

- Take a flight or ferry back to Athens for your departure.

Remember to check ferry and flight schedules in advance and plan accordingly. This itinerary offers a mix of history, culture, and island exploration, allowing you to experience the best of Athens and one or two stunning Greek islands within five days.

weekend itinerary

If you have a weekend to spend in Greece, it's best to focus on exploring Athens and its nearby attractions. Here's a suggested weekend itinerary:

Day 1: Athens

- As soon as you get there, you can begin exploring Athens.

- Visit the well-known Acropolis and have a look at its historic buildings, such as the Parthenon and the Temple of Athena Nike.

- Explore the old Plaka district, which is renowned for its quaint shops, tavernas, and small lanes.

- Explore the Ancient Agora, the heart of ancient Athens, where Socrates and Plato once walked.

- Enjoy a delicious Greek dinner at a local restaurant.

Day 2: Day trip to Cape Sounion

- Visit Cape Sounion for the day; it's around an hour's drive from Athens.

- Visit the Temple of Poseidon, which is positioned on a cliff above the Aegean Sea and offers stunning sunset views.

- Swim in the pristine seas and explore the local beaches.

- Once back in Athens, spend the evening taking advantage of the exciting nightlife the city has to offer, including the rooftop bars and live music venues.

Day 3: Athens

- Visit the National Archaeological Museum first thing in the morning, where there is a sizable collection of Greek artifacts.

- Discover the Monastiraki area, known for its thriving flea market and energetic ambiance.

- Wander through the lovely Anafiotika neighborhood, a little area with a Cycladic island feel that is situated beneath the Acropolis.

- If you want to learn more about Greek history and culture, go visit the Benaki Museum or the Museum of Cycladic Art.

- Take in the regional cuisine as you say goodbye over dinner at a traditional Greek tavern.

This weekend itinerary allows you to experience the highlights of Athens, including its ancient landmarks, historical neighborhoods, and vibrant culture. While there are many other destinations to explore in Greece, a weekend in Athens provides a taste of the country's rich history and warm hospitality.

Two weeks itinerary

Day 1-3: Athens

- Visit the Acropolis, the Parthenon, and the Ancient Agora, some of Athens' historical landmarks.

- Visit the National Archaeological Museum and the Acropolis Museum.

- Explore Athens' historic Plaka area by foot.

- Dine on Greek food in neighborhood taverns.

Day 4-5: Santorini

- Take a quick flight or a ferry to Santorini.

- Explore Oia, Fira, and Imerovigli, three stunning settlements.

- Visit the volcanic caldera to witness the mesmerizing sunsets.

- Unwind on the beaches with black sand.

- Go on a boat cruise to the surrounding islands of Nea Kameni and Thirassia, which is optional.

Day 6-7: Mykonos

- Take a quick flight or a ferry to Mykonos.

- Discover Chora's famous windmills (Mykonos Town).

- Unwind on Paradise and Super Paradise's beautiful beaches.

- Enjoy the exciting party scene and nightlife.

- Visit the adjacent UNESCO World Heritage site of Delos.

Day 8-10: Crete

- Take a quick flight or a ferry to Crete.

- Investigate the historical sites of Knossos Palace and the Heraklion Archaeological Museum.

- Visit Chania and Rethymno, two quaint historic towns.

- Visit the stunning beaches of Elafonisi and Balos or take a hike through the Samaria Gorge.

- Try local specialties and Cretan food.

Day 11-13: Rhodes

- travel to Rhodes by plane.

- Discover Rhodes' historic Old Town, a UNESCO World Heritage site.

- Visit the Street of the Knights and the Grand Master's Palace.

- Unwind in Lindos and Faliraki beaches.

- Visit the Valley of the Butterflies and the ancient city of Kamiros.

Day 14: Return to Athens

- Go back to Athens by air or ferry.

- Take the day to visit any missed sights or go souvenir shopping.

- In a typical Greek taverna, take pleasure in a farewell dinner.

Chapter 4: Best Restaurants and Cuisine

Greece is recognized for its extensive culinary history and wide range of tastes. The nation has a lot to offer in terms of dining experiences, from traditional tavernas serving authentic Greek food to sophisticated restaurants delivering modern interpretations of Mediterranean foods.

Greek food is well-known throughout the world for its mouthwatering flavors and vivid Mediterranean ingredients. Greece's regional specialties, herbs, olive oil, and fresh, seasonal products are all celebrated in the local cuisine. Here are some of the culinary highlights of Greece:

1. Olive Oil: Greece is one of the largest producers of olive oil, and it is a staple ingredient in Greek cuisine. It is used in almost every dish, from salads to cooked dishes, and is known for its exceptional quality.

2. Mezedes: Mezedes are a selection of small dishes that are often served as appetizers or shared plates. They include various dips like tzatziki (yogurt, cucumber, and garlic), melitzanosalata (eggplant dip), and taramasalata (fish roe dip). Other popular mezedes include dolmades (stuffed grape leaves), spanakopita (spinach and feta pastry), and saganaki (fried cheese).

3. Souvlaki and Gyro: Souvlaki and gyro are popular street food items in Greece. Souvlaki typically consists of grilled skewers of marinated meat, such as pork,

chicken, or lamb, served with pita bread, tzatziki, and garnishes. Gyro is made from seasoned meat (usually pork or chicken) cooked on a vertical rotisserie and served in a pita with various toppings.

4. Moussaka: Moussaka is a classic Greek dish made with layers of eggplant, minced meat (usually beef or lamb), and topped with a rich béchamel sauce. It is baked to perfection and is a hearty and flavorful dish.

5. Greek Salad: A traditional Greek salad, or horiatiki, is a refreshing combination of tomatoes, cucumbers, onions, peppers, olives, and feta cheese, dressed with olive oil and sprinkled with oregano. It's a staple in Greek cuisine and often served as a side dish or a light meal.

6. Fresh Seafood: With its extensive coastline, Greece offers an abundance of fresh seafood. Grilled octopus, fried calamari, baked fish, and prawn saganaki (prawns cooked in a tomato and feta sauce) are just a few examples of the delicious seafood dishes you can find.

7. Baklava: Baklava is a popular Greek dessert made of layers of filo pastry filled with a mixture of chopped nuts, sugar, and spices, soaked in sweet syrup. It is sweet, rich, and a perfect ending to a Greek meal.

8. Greek Wines: Greece has a long history of wine production, and Greek wines are gaining recognition globally. From crisp whites like Assyrtiko to robust reds

like Xinomavro, there is a wide range of Greek wines to explore and pair with your meal.

When it comes to dining in Greece, visitors are spoiled for choice with an array of eatery joints offering delicious cuisine ranging from traditional Greek dishes to international fare. Here are some popular options for dining out in Greece:

1. **Tavernas:** Tavernas are traditional Greek eateries known for their casual and inviting atmosphere, where you can enjoy authentic Greek cuisine in a relaxed setting. These family-owned establishments serve classic dishes such as moussaka, souvlaki, Greek salad, grilled fish, and mezedes (small plates) accompanied by local wine or ouzo.

2. **Ouzeries:** Ouzeries specialize in serving ouzo, a traditional Greek spirit, along with mezedes (appetizers) and small plates. These cozy establishments are perfect for sampling a variety of Greek flavors, including olives, feta cheese, grilled octopus, tzatziki, and fried calamari, while sipping on ouzo or tsipouro.

3. **Psarotavernas:** Psarotavernas, or fish tavernas, are seafood restaurants typically located near the coast or fishing harbors, where you can enjoy freshly caught fish and seafood prepared in traditional Greek style. From grilled sardines and octopus to seafood risotto and fried calamari, psarotavernas offer a variety of seafood dishes to satisfy your cravings.

4. **Kafeneia:** Kafeneia are traditional Greek cafes where locals gather to socialize, sip coffee, and enjoy light snacks throughout the day. In addition to coffee, kafeneia serve pastries, sandwiches, and desserts, making them ideal for a quick breakfast or afternoon pick-me-up.

5. **Ouzeri-Mezedopoleia:** These establishments combine the concepts of ouzeri (ouzo bars) and mezedopoleia (meze restaurants), offering a wide selection of mezedes (small plates) to accompany your drinks. Enjoy a leisurely meal of grilled meats, seafood, salads, and dips while sipping on ouzo, wine, or beer.

6. **Restaurants:** Greece is home to a diverse range of restaurants catering to various tastes and preferences, from fine dining establishments serving gourmet cuisine to casual eateries offering international fare. Whether you're craving Italian pasta, Asian fusion, or American burgers, you'll find plenty of restaurant options in urban centers and tourist areas.

7. **Bakeries and Pastry Shops:** Indulge your sweet tooth at Greek bakeries and pastry shops, where you can sample an array of freshly baked goods, including baklava, loukoumades (honey dumplings), bougatsa (custard-filled pastry), and koulouri (sesame bread rings). Pair your pastries with a Greek coffee or frappe for a delicious treat.

8. **Street Food Stalls:** Explore the vibrant street food scene in Greece, where you can find savory and sweet snacks sold from food stalls and carts in busy markets and tourist areas. Try classic street foods like souvlaki (grilled meat skewers), gyros (meat wrapped in pita bread), koulouri (sesame bread rings), and loukoumades (fried dough balls drizzled with honey).

Whether you're dining in a traditional taverna, savoring seafood at a psarotaverna, or indulging in street food delights, eating out in Greece is a culinary adventure that promises to delight your taste buds and immerse you in the rich flavors of Greek cuisine.

While it's challenging to narrow down the list to just a few, here are some of the **best restaurants in Greece** that are highly recommended:

1. Funky Gourmet (Athens): This Michelin-starred restaurant in Athens offers an innovative tasting menu that combines Greek ingredients with modern cooking techniques. With its artistic presentations and bold flavors, Funky Gourmet provides a unique gastronomic experience.

2. Argo (Santorini): Located in the picturesque village of Fira, Argo is known for its breathtaking views of the caldera and sunset. This family-run restaurant

specializes in fresh seafood dishes, including grilled fish and traditional Greek mezes.

3. Kritamon (Chania, Crete): Situated in the charming Old Town of Chania, Kritamon showcases Cretan cuisine at its finest. The menu features locally sourced ingredients, highlighting the island's renowned olive oil, herbs, and cheeses.

4. Spondi (Athens): Another Michelin-starred establishment, Spondi is considered one of the best fine-dining restaurants in Athens. Its elegant ambiance and impeccable service complement the exquisite French-inspired Mediterranean dishes on offer.

5. Selene (Santorini): Located in the village of Pyrgos, Selene is a long-established restaurant that celebrates the flavors of Santorini and the Cycladic region. The menu focuses on seasonal ingredients and traditional recipes, ensuring an authentic taste of the island.

6. Ta Karamanlidika Tou Fani (Athens): For a more casual dining experience, Ta Karamanlidika Tou Fani is a must-visit. This deli and restaurant in the heart of Athens offers a selection of cured meats, cheeses, and other Greek delicacies, perfect for a quick lunch or a relaxed evening meal.

7. To Palio Hamam (Thessaloniki): Housed in a converted Ottoman-era bathhouse, To Palio Hamam offers a blend of traditional and modern Greek cuisine. The

restaurant is known for its creative dishes, cozy atmosphere, and live music performances.

8. Varoulko (Athens): As a pioneer of seafood cuisine in Greece, Varoulko holds a prominent place in the culinary scene. Located in Mikrolimano Marina, this Michelin-starred restaurant presents beautifully crafted seafood dishes with a contemporary twist.

9. Avli (Rethymno, Crete): Avli is situated in a stunning courtyard in Rethymno's old town and offers a combination of Cretan and Mediterranean cuisine. The restaurant's warm ambiance and flavorsome dishes make it a popular choice among locals and visitors alike.

10. Dexamenes Seaside Hotel (Kourouta Beach, Peloponnese): While not strictly a restaurant, Dexamenes Seaside Hotel deserves a mention for its unique dining experience. This boutique hotel in a renovated wine factory provides guests with the opportunity to enjoy delicious food and local wines while admiring the stunning sunset over the Ionian Sea.

Chapter 5: Accommodations in Greece

Greece offers a diverse range of accommodation options to suit every budget, travel style, and preference. Whether you're seeking luxury resorts, boutique hotels, charming guesthouses, or budget-friendly hostels, Greece has something for everyone. Here are some popular accommodation options in Greece:

1. **Luxury Resorts and Hotels:**

   - Greece boasts an abundance of luxury resorts and hotels located in stunning coastal settings, offering upscale amenities, personalized service, and breathtaking views of the Aegean and Ionian Seas. From beachfront resorts in Santorini and Mykonos to luxury villas in Crete and luxury boutique hotels in Athens, luxury travelers can indulge in opulent accommodations and world-class hospitality.

2. **Boutique Hotels and Guesthouses:**

   - Boutique hotels and guesthouses are intimate and stylish accommodations that offer a unique and personalized experience. Often located in historic buildings or traditional villages, boutique hotels in Greece feature charming architecture, chic decor, and attentive service. These properties provide a cozy and romantic atmosphere, perfect for couples and travelers seeking a more intimate stay.

3. **Traditional Villas and Houses:**

- Experience Greek hospitality in a traditional villa or house, where you can enjoy the comforts of home while immersing yourself in the local culture and lifestyle. Many villas and houses in Greece feature traditional architecture, rustic furnishings, and modern amenities, making them ideal for families, groups, or long-term stays. Renting a villa or house allows you to enjoy privacy, space, and flexibility during your visit.

4. **Apartment Rentals and Vacation Homes:**

- Apartment rentals and vacation homes are popular accommodation options for travelers seeking independence, flexibility, and affordability. Whether you're staying in a city apartment in Athens, a beachfront condo in Corfu, or a countryside cottage in Pelion, renting an apartment or vacation home allows you to live like a local and experience Greece at your own pace.

5. **Budget-Friendly Hostels and Guesthouses:**

- Budget-conscious travelers can find affordable accommodation options in Greece, including hostels, guesthouses, and budget hotels. These properties offer basic amenities, shared or private rooms, and communal spaces for socializing and meeting fellow travelers. Hostels are particularly popular among backpackers, solo travelers, and young adventurers looking to explore Greece on a budget.

6. **Camping and Glamping Sites:**

- For nature lovers and outdoor enthusiasts, Greece offers a variety of camping and glamping sites in scenic locations across the country. From beachside campsites in the Greek islands to mountain retreats in the mainland, camping and glamping provide an immersive and adventurous way to experience Greece's natural beauty and landscapes.

7. **Agritourism and Eco-Friendly Lodgings:**

- Experience sustainable tourism practices and eco-friendly accommodations in Greece by staying at agritourism farms, eco-lodges, and nature retreats. These properties offer a unique opportunity to connect with nature, learn about traditional farming practices, and support local communities while enjoying comfortable and environmentally conscious accommodations.

Whether you're seeking luxury and relaxation, cultural immersion, or budget-friendly options, Greece offers a wide range of accommodation choices to suit every traveler's needs and preferences. From coastal resorts and boutique hotels to traditional villas and budget-friendly hostels, finding the perfect place to stay in Greece is part of the adventure of exploring this beautiful and diverse country.

Here are a few of Greece's top hotels for lodging:

1. Amanzoe, Porto Heli: Located in the Peloponnese region, Amanzoe is a luxurious resort offering private villas with stunning sea views. The hotel features a private beach, a world-class spa, a fitness center, and an infinity pool. Guests can enjoy personalized services, including a private chef, butler, and chauffeur.

2. Canaves Oia, Santorini: Situated in the picturesque village of Oia, Canaves Oia is a boutique hotel famous for its stunning views of the Caldera. The hotel offers elegant suites and villas with private pools or plunge pools. Guests can enjoy amenities such as a gourmet restaurant, a spa, a wine cellar, and a rooftop infinity pool.

3. Eagles Palace, Halkidiki: Located in the region of Halkidiki, Eagles Palace is a luxury beachfront hotel offering elegant rooms, suites, and bungalows with sea or garden views. The hotel boasts a private sandy beach, a spa center, a kids' club, multiple restaurants, and a water sports center.

4. Bill & Coo Suites and Lounge, Mykonos: Situated in Mykonos town, Bill & Coo is a boutique hotel known for its contemporary design and impeccable service. The hotel offers luxurious suites with private pools or hot

tubs. Guests can enjoy a gourmet restaurant, a stylish lounge bar, a spa, and a stunning infinity pool overlooking the Aegean Sea.

5. Costa Navarino, Messinia: Located in the Peloponnese, Costa Navarino is a luxury resort complex offering two 5-star hotels: The Romanos and The Westin Resort Costa Navarino. The resort features spacious rooms and suites, multiple restaurants, golf courses, a spa, sports facilities, and access to private beaches.

6. Grace Santorini, Santorini: Perched on a cliffside in Santorini, Grace Santorini is a boutique hotel known for its minimalist design and breathtaking views of the Caldera. The hotel offers stylish suites with private plunge pools or hot tubs. Guests can enjoy a gourmet restaurant, a champagne lounge, and a spa.

7. Domes of Elounda, Crete: Situated in Elounda, Crete, Domes of Elounda is a luxury resort offering spacious suites, villas, and residences with private pools or hot tubs. The resort features a private sandy beach, multiple restaurants, a spa, a kids' club, and a variety of water sports activities. the resort provides a dedicated Kids Club with various activities and amenities to entertain young guests. The club offers supervised programs and age-appropriate facilities, ensuring that children have a fun and enjoyable stay.

Chapter 6: Cultural Activities in Greece

Greek culture is a rich tapestry woven from thousands of years of history, tradition, and diversity. Influenced by ancient civilizations, including the Minoans, Mycenaeans, and Greeks, as well as Byzantine, Ottoman, and modern European cultures, Greek culture is a blend of classical heritage, Orthodox Christianity, Mediterranean lifestyle, and contemporary influences.

Greece is the birthplace of Western civilization, known for its contributions to philosophy, literature, art, architecture, and democracy. Ancient Greek achievements, such as the development of democracy, theater, and philosophy by figures like Plato, Aristotle, and Sophocles, continue to inspire and influence global culture.

Here are 20 cultural activities that visitors can enjoy in Greece:

1. **Visit the Acropolis:** Explore the iconic Acropolis in Athens, a UNESCO World Heritage Site, and marvel at ancient architectural masterpieces such as the Parthenon, Erechtheion, and Temple of Athena Nike.

2. **Discover Ancient Delphi:** Journey to the archaeological site of Delphi, home to the ancient Oracle of Delphi and the impressive ruins of the Temple of Apollo, theater, and stadium.

3. **Experience Greek Theater:** Attend a performance at an ancient theater, such as the Theater of Epidaurus

or the Odeon of Herodes Atticus in Athens, and immerse yourself in the timeless art of Greek drama.

4. **Participate in Greek Dance:** Learn traditional Greek dances such as syrtaki, zeibekiko, and kalamatianó at a local taverna or dance workshop, and join in the spirited festivities of Greek music and dance.

5. **Celebrate Greek Easter:** Experience the vibrant celebrations of Greek Orthodox Easter, including religious processions, church services, feasting on traditional Easter dishes, and cracking red eggs for good luck.

6. **Explore Monastic Meteora:** Visit the UNESCO-listed monasteries of Meteora, perched atop towering rock formations in central Greece, and admire their breathtaking architecture, religious icons, and panoramic views.

7. **Sample Greek Cuisine:** Indulge in the flavors of Greek cuisine by sampling traditional dishes such as moussaka, souvlaki, spanakopita, and baklava at local tavernas, markets, and food festivals.

8. **Attend a Greek Festival:** Experience the lively atmosphere of Greek festivals and cultural events, including music festivals, religious feasts, and wine festivals, where you can enjoy live music, dance, and gastronomic delights.

9. **Explore Byzantine Monuments:** Discover the legacy of the Byzantine Empire by visiting Byzantine

churches, monasteries, and frescoes in cities like Thessaloniki, Mystras, and Ioannina.

10. **Learn about Greek Mythology:** Delve into the world of Greek mythology at archaeological sites such as Olympia, Corinth, and Knossos, and learn about legendary gods, heroes, and myths that have shaped Greek culture and identity.

11. **Visit Ancient Olympia:** Explore the birthplace of the Olympic Games at the archaeological site of Olympia, where you can see the remains of ancient stadiums, temples, and athletic facilities.

12. **Discover Minoan Civilization:** Explore the ancient palace of Knossos on the island of Crete, the center of the Minoan civilization, and marvel at its intricate architecture, colorful frescoes, and mythical labyrinth.

13. **Experience Greek Music:** Attend a live performance of traditional Greek music, including bouzouki, lyra, and laouto, at a local taverna, concert hall, or outdoor venue.

14. **Admire Byzantine Art:** Visit museums and galleries to admire Byzantine art and artifacts, including religious icons, mosaics, and manuscripts, showcasing the artistic legacy of the Byzantine Empire.

15. **Discover Ancient Sparta:** Explore the ruins of ancient Sparta at archaeological sites such as Mystras and Sparta, and learn about the history and culture of this legendary city-state.

16. **Learn Greek Calligraphy:** Take a workshop in Greek calligraphy (caligraphy), known as "kalligrafía," and learn the art of writing Greek letters in various styles, including Byzantine script and modern Greek handwriting.

17. **Attend a Greek Wedding:** Experience the joy and traditions of a Greek wedding ceremony, including the exchange of vows, crowning of the bride and groom, traditional dances, and festive feasting.

18. **Explore Ancient Corinth:** Visit the archaeological site of ancient Corinth, where you can explore ruins such as the Temple of Apollo, the Agora, and the Roman Forum, and learn about the city's role in ancient Greek history.

19. **Take a Cooking Class:** Learn to cook traditional Greek dishes from local chefs and culinary experts during a cooking class or culinary tour, and discover the secrets of Greek cuisine using fresh, seasonal ingredients.

20. **Sail the Greek Islands:** Embark on a sailing adventure to explore the Greek islands, hopping from one picturesque island to another, swimming in crystal-clear waters, and experiencing the laid-back lifestyle of island living.

These cultural activities offer visitors a unique opportunity to immerse themselves in the rich history, traditions, and heritage of Greece while creating unforgettable memories of their travels in this beautiful country.

Chapter 7: Nightlife And Festivals In Greece

Greece's nightlife scene is vibrant and diverse, offering something for everyone, from chic rooftop bars with stunning views to lively beach clubs pulsating with music and energy. Here are ten must-visit night destinations in Greece, along with renowned joints and activities to enjoy:

1. **Athens:**

   - **Baba Au Rum:** Located in the heart of Athens, Baba Au Rum is a renowned cocktail bar known for its creative concoctions and cozy ambiance. Enjoy expertly crafted cocktails made with premium spirits and fresh ingredients in a stylish setting.

   - **Gazi District:** Explore the Gazi district, known for its lively nightlife scene with bars, clubs, and restaurants housed in renovated industrial buildings. Dance the night away at clubs like BIOS, where you can enjoy live music, DJ sets, and cultural events.

2. **Thessaloniki:**

   - **Ladadika:** Wander through the historic Ladadika district, lined with traditional tavernas, bars, and cafes. Sample local mezedes (small plates) and ouzo while soaking up the vibrant atmosphere of this bustling neighborhood.

- **Valaoritou Street:** Experience Thessaloniki's nightlife on Valaoritou Street, home to hip bars, cocktail lounges, and nightclubs. Join the stylish crowd at places like TORA K44 for signature cocktails and DJ sets that keep the party going until the early hours.

3. **Mykonos:**

- **Paradise Beach Club:** Spend an unforgettable night at Paradise Beach Club, one of Mykonos' legendary beach clubs known for its electrifying parties and international DJs. Dance barefoot in the sand, sip cocktails by the sea, and enjoy live performances and themed events under the stars.

- **Little Venice:** Explore the picturesque neighborhood of Little Venice, where charming cafes and bars overlook the sea, offering stunning sunset views and a romantic atmosphere. Relax with a cocktail at Caprice Bar as you watch the waves crash against the shoreline.

4. **Santorini:**

- **Fira Town:** Discover the nightlife of Fira Town, Santorini's bustling capital, where you'll find a mix of bars, clubs, and tavernas lining the narrow streets. Enjoy sunset cocktails at PK

Cocktail Bar, perched on the edge of the caldera with panoramic views of the Aegean Sea.

- **Kamari Beach:** Experience a beachside party at Kamari Beach, where beach bars like Wet Stories and Sea Side by Notos offer DJ sets, live music, and dancing under the stars. Lounge on sunbeds, sip cocktails, and soak up the laid-back vibe of Santorini's famous black sand beach.

5. **Rhodes:**

- **Rhodes Town:** Dive into the nightlife of Rhodes Town, where medieval charm meets modern entertainment. Explore the labyrinthine streets of the Old Town and discover hidden bars and cafes tucked away in historic buildings.

- **Faliraki:** Experience the lively atmosphere of Faliraki, Rhodes' party hub known for its beachfront bars and clubs. Join the fun at venues like Bed Club and Liquid Club, where international DJs, themed parties, and beach parties keep the energy high all night long.

6. **Crete:**

- **Heraklion:** Enjoy a night out in Heraklion, Crete's vibrant capital, where you'll find a mix of traditional tavernas, modern bars, and music venues. Head to 7 Thalasses for cocktails and live music overlooking the old Venetian harbor.

- **Hersonissos:** Party until dawn in Hersonissos, Crete's premier nightlife destination, where beach clubs like Star Beach and Ammos Beach Club host epic parties with DJs, water sports, and foam parties.

7. **Corfu:**

- **Corfu Town:** Experience the nightlife of Corfu Town, where historic charm meets contemporary entertainment. Explore the narrow streets of the Old Town and discover rooftop bars, jazz clubs, and wine bars offering live music and local wines.

- **Kavos:** Dive into the party scene of Kavos, Corfu's lively resort town known for its beach parties and vibrant nightlife. Dance until sunrise at famous clubs like Future Club and Atlantis Club, where international DJs and themed events keep the crowds entertained.

8. **Zakynthos (Zante):**

- **Laganas:** Discover the nightlife of Laganas, Zakynthos' party capital, where beachfront bars and clubs line the sandy shores. Join the fun at venues like Rescue Club and Cocktails & Dreams for foam parties, DJ sets, and beachside cocktails.

- **Zakynthos Town:** Experience a more laid-back vibe in Zakynthos Town, where waterfront cafes and bars offer views of the marina and harbor. Sip cocktails at Boheme Bar and enjoy live music and chill-out vibes in a relaxed setting.

9. **Naxos:**

- **Naxos Town:** Explore the nightlife of Naxos Town, where you'll find a mix of traditional tavernas, cocktail bars, and music venues. Relax with a drink at Naxos Blue Bar and enjoy live jazz, blues, and rock performances in a cozy atmosphere.

- **Agia Anna Beach:** Experience a beach party at Agia Anna Beach, where beach bars like Banana Beach Bar and Island Bar host sunset parties, DJ sets, and bonfires on the sand.

10. **Paros:**

- **Naoussa:** Discover the nightlife of Naoussa, Paros' picturesque fishing village, where chic bars and waterfront tavernas line the harbor. Sip cocktails at Barbarossa Bar and enjoy sunset views and chill-out music in a stylish setting.

- **Punda Beach:** Dance the night away at Punda Beach Club, one of Paros' top beach clubs known for its lively parties and international DJs. Enjoy beach volleyball, water sports, and themed events during the day, then dance under the stars until dawn.

These must-visit night destinations in Greece offer an unforgettable mix of music, dancing, cocktails, and atmosphere, ensuring a memorable and exhilarating nightlife experience for visitors from around the world.

Festivals

Greece is known for its vibrant festival culture, with celebrations happening throughout the year to mark religious, cultural, and seasonal occasions. Here are 20 festivals to enjoy in Greece, along with when they occur and the activities they offer:

1. **Apokries (Carnival):** Held in February or March, Apokries is Greece's carnival season, celebrated with colorful parades, masquerade parties, and street festivities. Join locals in costume parades, traditional dances, and feasts before the start of Lent.

2. **Greek Independence Day:** Celebrated on March 25th, Greek Independence Day commemorates Greece's declaration of independence from the Ottoman Empire in 1821. Festivities include military parades, school performances, and patriotic ceremonies.

3. **Easter:** Easter is one of the most significant religious holidays in Greece, celebrated with solemn processions, church services, and festive feasting. Experience Holy Week traditions, including the Epitaphios procession on Good Friday and midnight Easter services on Holy Saturday.

4. **Athens Epidaurus Festival:** From June to August, the Athens Epidaurus Festival showcases theater, music, dance, and cultural events at iconic venues such as the Odeon of Herodes Atticus and the Ancient Theater of Epidaurus. Enjoy performances ranging from ancient Greek tragedies to modern theater productions.

5. **International Music Day (World Music Day):** Celebrated on June 21st, International Music Day brings music to the streets and squares of Greek cities and towns, with free concerts, jam sessions, and musical performances by local and international artists.

6. **Rethymno Renaissance Festival:** Held in July and August, the Rethymno Renaissance Festival in Crete celebrates the island's Venetian heritage with Renaissance-themed events, including concerts, art exhibitions, theater performances, and historical reenactments.

7. **Rockwave Festival:** Taking place in July, the Rockwave Festival is Greece's largest rock music festival, featuring performances by Greek and international bands across multiple stages. Enjoy three days of live music, camping, and outdoor fun at Terra Vibe Park near Athens.

8. **Thessaloniki International Film Festival:** Held in November, the Thessaloniki International Film Festival is one of Europe's leading film festivals, showcasing a

diverse selection of Greek and international films, documentaries, and shorts. Attend screenings, Q&A sessions, and special events across the city.

9. **Ohi Day (Anniversary of Greek Resistance):** Celebrated on October 28th, Ohi Day commemorates Greece's refusal to surrender to Axis forces during World War II. Festivities include military parades, school celebrations, and patriotic ceremonies honoring Greek heroes.

10. **Feast of St. Nicholas:** Celebrated on December 6th, the Feast of St. Nicholas honors the patron saint of sailors and fishermen. Coastal towns and islands hold religious processions, boat blessings, and seafood feasts to commemorate the occasion.

11. **Santorini International Music Festival:** Held in September, the Santorini International Music Festival brings classical music to the island's stunning venues, including churches, wineries, and open-air theaters. Enjoy performances by renowned musicians against the backdrop of Santorini's iconic scenery.

12. **Saronic Chamber Music Festival:** Taking place in July and August, the Saronic Chamber Music Festival offers chamber music concerts in picturesque venues across the Saronic Islands, including Hydra, Spetses, and Poros. Experience world-class performances by acclaimed musicians in intimate settings.

13. **Patras Carnival:** Held in January and February, the Patras Carnival is one of Greece's largest and most colorful carnivals, featuring parades, floats, and street parties. Join in the festivities with costume contests, music, dancing, and traditional Greek food and drinks.

14. **Chios Rocket War:** Taking place on Easter Saturday, the Chios Rocket War is a unique Easter tradition on the island of Chios, where two rival church congregations in the villages of Vrontados and Agios Markos launch homemade rockets at each other's church bell towers in a symbolic "war."

15. **Rhodes Medieval Festival:** Held in May, the Rhodes Medieval Festival celebrates the island's medieval heritage with historical reenactments, knight tournaments, and medieval-themed events. Explore the medieval city of Rhodes and experience life in the Middle Ages.

16. **Samos Wine Festival:** Taking place in August, the Samos Wine Festival celebrates the island's winemaking traditions with wine tastings, grape stomping, and cultural events. Sample a variety of local wines, enjoy live music, and experience the hospitality of Samos.

17. **Nafplio Festival:** From June to September, the Nafplio Festival hosts a series of cultural events, including concerts, theater performances, and art exhibitions, in the picturesque town of Nafplio.

Experience the rich cultural heritage of the Peloponnese in a charming setting.

18. **Meteora Summer Music Festival:** Held in July and August, the Meteora Summer Music Festival brings classical music to the breathtaking backdrop of the Meteora rock formations. Attend concerts in ancient monasteries and churches, and experience the magic of music in this UNESCO World Heritage Site.

19. **Crete Wine Festival:** Taking place in July and August, the Crete Wine Festival celebrates the island's winemaking tradition with wine tastings, vineyard tours, and cultural events. Discover the diverse wines of Crete and enjoy traditional Cretan music and dance.

20. **Zagori Mountain Running Festival:** Held in July, the Zagori Mountain Running Festival offers trail running races and outdoor activities in the stunning landscapes of the Zagori region in northern Greece. Join runners from around the world for a challenging and scenic mountain running experience.

These festivals offer visitors a unique opportunity to immerse themselves in Greek culture, traditions, and celebrations while experiencing the country's rich heritage and hospitality. Whether you're exploring ancient ruins, enjoying live music performances, or sampling local cuisine and wine, Greece's festivals promise unforgettable experiences and memories to treasure.

Chapter 8: Souvenirs And Shopping in Greece

Shopping in Greece is a delightful experience, blending traditional markets, modern shopping centers, and quaint boutiques offering a wide range of goods, from local handicrafts and souvenirs to designer fashion and artisanal products. Here's an overview of shopping life in Greece, followed by descriptions of the top ten shopping destinations and tips for a successful shopping experience:

Shopping Life in Greece:

Greece offers diverse shopping opportunities to cater to every taste and budget. In major cities like Athens and Thessaloniki, you'll find bustling shopping districts, luxury boutiques, and department stores, while picturesque islands boast charming shops selling local crafts, jewelry, and souvenirs. Greek shopping culture combines the convenience of modern malls with the charm of traditional markets, where bargaining and haggling are part of the experience. From open-air markets and artisan workshops to high-end designer boutiques and international brands, shopping in Greece is a rewarding and enjoyable activity for visitors and locals alike.

Top Ten Shopping Destinations in Greece:

1. **Ermou Street, Athens:** One of Athens' main shopping thoroughfares, Ermou Street is lined with shops, boutiques, and department stores offering clothing, accessories, and souvenirs. Explore

international brands, Greek designers, and local artisans while enjoying the vibrant atmosphere of central Athens.

2. **Plaka, Athens:** Wander through the historic neighborhood of Plaka, known for its charming streets lined with souvenir shops, artisanal boutiques, and traditional Greek handicrafts. Discover handmade jewelry, ceramics, textiles, and other unique treasures while soaking up the ambiance of ancient Athens.

3. **Monastiraki Flea Market, Athens:** Browse through the stalls of Monastiraki Flea Market, where you'll find a eclectic mix of antiques, vintage clothing, artwork, and souvenirs. Haggle with vendors, sample street food, and enjoy panoramic views of the Acropolis from this bustling market area.

4. **Golden Hall, Athens:** Indulge in luxury shopping at Golden Hall, one of Athens' premier shopping malls, featuring upscale boutiques, designer stores, and international brands. Explore fashion, beauty, and lifestyle products in a sophisticated and stylish environment.

5. **Tsimiski Street, Thessaloniki:** Explore Tsimiski Street, Thessaloniki's main shopping boulevard, lined with department stores, fashion boutiques, and specialty shops. Discover Greek and international brands, trendy cafes, and cultural attractions along this bustling pedestrian street.

6. **Aristotelous Square, Thessaloniki:** Enjoy shopping with a view at Aristotelous Square, Thessaloniki's central square overlooking the sea. Stroll along the waterfront promenade and browse through shops selling clothing, accessories, and souvenirs while admiring the city's neoclassical architecture.

7. **Chania Old Town, Crete:** Lose yourself in the maze of narrow streets and alleyways of Chania Old Town, where you'll find charming shops selling local crafts, handmade jewelry, leather goods, and traditional Cretan products. Explore hidden courtyards, artisan workshops, and quaint cafes in this atmospheric shopping district.

8. **Oia, Santorini:** Experience boutique shopping in the picturesque village of Oia, Santorini, known for its stunning sunset views and whitewashed buildings. Discover art galleries, jewelry shops, and upscale boutiques offering unique souvenirs and gifts with a backdrop of breathtaking scenery.

9. **Mykonos Town:** Shop till you drop in Mykonos Town, where chic boutiques, designer stores, and art galleries line the narrow streets of the Cycladic island. Browse through fashion, jewelry, and accessories while enjoying the cosmopolitan vibe of this popular shopping destination.

10. **Rhodes Old Town:** Step back in time in Rhodes Old Town, a UNESCO World Heritage Site famed for its

medieval architecture and charming shops. Explore the cobblestone streets and medieval alleys lined with artisan workshops, souvenir shops, and boutiques selling local crafts and products.

Tips for Shopping in Greece:

1. **Bring Cash:** While credit cards are widely accepted in larger stores and malls, smaller shops, markets, and street vendors may prefer cash. Make sure to carry small denominations and change for transactions.

2. **Bargain Wisely:** Bargaining is common in markets and flea markets, but be respectful and polite when negotiating prices. Start with a lower offer and be prepared to compromise for a fair deal.

3. **Shop Local:** Support local artisans and businesses by purchasing handmade products, traditional crafts, and locally sourced goods. Look for "Made in Greece" labels and seek out authentic Greek souvenirs to take home as mementos.

4. **Timing Matters:** Avoid shopping during peak hours and tourist crowds to enjoy a more relaxed and leisurely experience. Visit markets and shopping districts early in the morning or late in the afternoon for a quieter atmosphere.

5. **Explore Off the Beaten Path:** Venture beyond tourist areas and explore neighborhoods frequented by locals for unique shopping finds and authentic

experiences. Ask for recommendations from locals and shopkeepers for hidden gems and insider tips.

6. **Check Return Policies:** Before making a purchase, inquire about the store's return and exchange policies, especially for clothing, accessories, and souvenirs. Keep receipts and packaging in case you need to return or exchange items later.

7. **Stay Hydrated:** Shopping in Greece can be tiring, especially during the summer months, so remember to stay hydrated by carrying a reusable water bottle with you. Look for public water fountains or refill stations to stay refreshed while exploring.

8. **Plan Ahead:** Research shopping destinations and plan your itinerary in advance to make the most of your shopping experience in Greece. Prioritize must-visit shops, markets, and districts, and allow plenty of time for browsing and exploration.

9. **Learn Some Greek Phrases:** Brush up on basic Greek phrases and greetings to communicate with shopkeepers and locals. Even simple phrases like "hello" (γειά σας) and "thank you" (ευχαριστώ) can go a long way in making connections and showing appreciation.

10. **Enjoy the Experience:** Shopping in Greece is not just about purchasing goods—it's about immersing yourself in the culture, meeting local artisans, and discovering the stories behind the products. Take your time, savor

the experience, and enjoy the sights, sounds, and flavors of Greek shopping life.

Souvenirs

Here are 20 popular souvenirs to buy in Greece and where to find them:

1. **Olive Oil:** Look for extra virgin olive oil, a staple of Greek cuisine, available in specialty shops, markets, and supermarkets throughout Greece. Regions like Crete and Peloponnese are renowned for their high-quality olive oil.

2. **Olive Wood Products:** Purchase handmade olive wood products such as cutting boards, utensils, and decorative items from artisan workshops and souvenir shops in olive-growing regions like Crete, Zakynthos, and Kalamata.

3. **Greek Honey:** Sample and purchase Greek honey, known for its rich flavor and therapeutic properties, from local beekeepers, honey farms, and gourmet food stores across Greece. Look for varieties such as thyme, pine, and wildflower honey.

4. **Traditional Greek Sweets:** Indulge in traditional Greek sweets like baklava, loukoumades (honey-soaked doughnuts), and spoon sweets (preserved fruit in syrup), available in bakeries, sweet shops, and markets throughout Greece.

5. **Greek Wines:** Discover Greek wines from indigenous grape varieties such as Assyrtiko, Agiorgitiko, and Xinomavro, available for tasting and purchase at wineries, wine shops, and specialty stores in wine-producing regions like Santorini, Nemea, and Naoussa.

6. **Handmade Ceramics:** Browse through pottery workshops and artisan studios in villages like Margarites in Crete, Souroti in Thessaloniki, and Skopelos in the Sporades to find handcrafted ceramics, including vases, bowls, and decorative items.

7. **Traditional Greek Textiles:** Shop for traditional Greek textiles such as handwoven rugs, blankets, and table linens in markets, souvenir shops, and textile cooperatives in regions like Metsovo in Epirus, Ioannina in Epirus, and Naxos in the Cyclades.

8. **Komboloi (Worry Beads):** Purchase komboloi, strands of worry beads used for relaxation and stress relief, from specialty shops, souvenir stalls, and flea markets in cities like Athens, Thessaloniki, and Rhodes.

9. **Greek Spices and Herbs:** Stock up on Greek spices and herbs such as oregano, thyme, and sage from spice shops, markets, and delis across Greece. Look for locally sourced and organically grown herbs for authentic Greek flavors.

10. **Icon Replicas:** Find replica icons of Greek Orthodox religious icons depicting saints, angels, and religious

scenes in souvenir shops, monasteries, and religious stores in cities like Athens, Mykonos, and Meteora.

11. **Traditional Greek Costumes:** Purchase miniature replicas of traditional Greek costumes, including tsolias (men's outfit) and foustanella (men's skirt) for souvenirs and gifts from specialty shops and souvenir stores in tourist areas.

12. **Greek Olives and Olive Products:** Taste and buy a variety of Greek olives, olive paste, and olive-based skincare products from olive groves, farmers' markets, and specialty stores in regions like Kalamata in the Peloponnese and Crete.

13. **Greek Cheeses:** Sample and purchase Greek cheeses such as feta, graviera, and kefalotyri from cheese shops, dairy farms, and markets across Greece. Look for PDO (Protected Designation of Origin) cheeses for authentic flavors.

14. **Greek Sea Sponges:** Browse through seaside shops and souvenir stalls in coastal towns and islands like Symi, Kalymnos, and Hydra to find natural sea sponges harvested from the Aegean Sea for bathing and exfoliation.

15. **Evil Eye Talismans:** Ward off the evil eye with talismans and charms featuring the blue eye symbol, believed to protect against negative energy and bring good luck. Find evil eye souvenirs in gift shops, markets, and jewelry stores across Greece.

16. **Greek Leather Sandals:** Purchase handmade leather sandals, a staple of Greek summer fashion, from shoemakers, boutique shops, and open-air markets in Athens, Mykonos, and Santorini. Choose from traditional designs or modern styles in various colors.

17. **Greek Coffee and Briki:** Enjoy Greek coffee, a strong and flavorful brew served in small cups, and purchase a briki (coffee pot) for brewing at home from coffee shops, supermarkets, and specialty stores in Greece.

18. **Greek Musical Instruments:** Discover traditional Greek musical instruments such as bouzouki, baglamas, and tzouras in music shops, souvenir stores, and markets in Athens, Thessaloniki, and Crete.

19. **Kalamata Fig Preserves:** Taste and buy Kalamata fig preserves, a sweet delicacy made from local figs, from gourmet food shops, farmers' markets, and specialty stores in Kalamata and Messinia.

20. **Greek Jewelry:** Adorn yourself with Greek jewelry inspired by ancient motifs and symbols, including meander patterns, olive branches, and Greek gods. Find handmade jewelry in gold, silver, and semi-precious stones in jewelry stores and boutiques across Greece.

These souvenirs capture the essence of Greek culture, craftsmanship, and culinary heritage, allowing you to bring home a piece of Greece to cherish and share with others.

Chapter 9: Tips For Traveling in Greece

Here are time-saving, money-saving, and general tips for traveling to Greece:

Time-Saving Tips:

1. **Plan Ahead:** Research your destinations, activities, and accommodations in advance to optimize your itinerary and make the most of your time in Greece.

2. **Use Public Transportation:** Take advantage of Greece's efficient public transportation system, including buses, trains, and ferries, to explore cities and islands without wasting time in traffic or searching for parking.

3. **Skip the Lines:** Purchase skip-the-line tickets for popular attractions and landmarks such as the Acropolis and archaeological sites to avoid long queues and save time during your visits.

4. **Visit Early or Late:** Arrive at popular tourist sites early in the morning or later in the afternoon to beat the crowds and enjoy a more relaxed experience without the rush.

5. **Use Mobile Apps:** Download travel apps for navigation, language translation, and local recommendations to help you save time and navigate unfamiliar surroundings more efficiently.

6. **Stay Central:** Choose accommodations in central locations close to major attractions, transportation hubs, and dining options to minimize travel time and maximize sightseeing opportunities.

7. **Pack Light:** Pack essentials and travel light to avoid wasting time waiting for luggage, navigating crowded streets, and carrying heavy bags during your travels.

Money-Saving Tips:

1. **Travel Off-Season:** Visit Greece during the shoulder seasons of spring and fall to take advantage of lower prices on flights, accommodations, and activities while still enjoying pleasant weather and fewer crowds.

2. **Eat Like a Local:** Dine at local tavernas, bakeries, and markets to experience authentic Greek cuisine at affordable prices. Look for daily specials and set menus for budget-friendly dining options.

3. **Stay in Budget Accommodations:** Opt for budget-friendly accommodations such as hostels, guesthouses, and rental apartments to save money on lodging while still enjoying comfortable and convenient stays.

4. **Shop at Markets:** Shop for fresh produce, snacks, and souvenirs at local markets and supermarkets rather than touristy shops to find better prices and support the local economy.

5. **Use Free Activities:** Take advantage of free activities and attractions such as visiting parks, beaches, and

historic sites, attending cultural events, and exploring walking trails to enjoy Greece without breaking the bank.

6. **Avoid Tourist Traps:** Be wary of tourist traps such as overpriced restaurants, souvenir shops, and guided tours in popular tourist areas, and seek out authentic and affordable alternatives off the beaten path.

7. **Book in Advance:** Book flights, accommodations, and activities in advance to secure lower prices and take advantage of early booking discounts and special promotions.

General Tips:

1. **Respect Local Customs:** Familiarize yourself with Greek customs and etiquette, including greeting locals with a friendly "kalimera" (good morning) or "kalispera" (good evening) and respecting cultural traditions and religious customs.

2. **Stay Hydrated:** Drink plenty of water, especially during the summer months, to stay hydrated and avoid dehydration while exploring Greece's sunny and warm climate.

3. **Protect Against Sun Exposure:** Wear sunscreen, sunglasses, and a hat to protect yourself from the sun's harmful rays while spending time outdoors, especially during peak sun hours from 10 am to 4 pm.

4. **Be Prepared for Weather:** Pack clothing and accessories suitable for Greece's Mediterranean climate, including lightweight and breathable fabrics for hot summers and layers for cooler evenings and shoulder seasons.

5. **Learn Basic Greek Phrases:** Learn basic Greek phrases and greetings to communicate with locals and show respect for the Greek language and culture. Even simple phrases like "efharisto" (thank you) and "parakalo" (please) can go a long way in making connections.

6. **Stay Safe:** Practice common sense safety precautions such as safeguarding your belongings, avoiding isolated areas at night, and staying informed about local safety alerts and guidelines.

7. **Embrace Slow Travel:** Allow yourself time to slow down, relax, and soak in the beauty and culture of Greece at a leisurely pace, rather than rushing from one attraction to another. Take time to savor local flavors, connect with locals, and create meaningful experiences that will last a lifetime.

By following these time-saving, money-saving, and general tips, you can make the most of your travels to Greece and create unforgettable memories while exploring this beautiful and historic destination.

Conclusion

In conclusion, embarking on a journey to Greece promises an adventure steeped in history, mythology, and unparalleled beauty. From the majestic ruins of ancient civilizations to the vibrant energy of modern cities and the idyllic charm of island paradises, Greece offers a tapestry of experiences that captivate the senses and enrich the soul.

As you traverse this land of legends and lore, immerse yourself in the timeless traditions of Greek hospitality, where strangers are welcomed as friends and every meal is an opportunity for connection and camaraderie. Explore the cobblestone streets of ancient towns, where echoes of the past mingle with the rhythms of everyday life, and discover hidden gems tucked away in picturesque villages and sun-drenched islands.

Indulge in the flavors of Mediterranean cuisine, savoring the freshness of locally sourced ingredients and the richness of centuries-old recipes passed down through generations. From tangy feta cheese and succulent olives to fragrant herbs and sweet honey, each bite tells a story of a land nourished by sun, sea, and soil.

As you navigate the bustling streets of Athens, the winding alleyways of island towns, and the tranquil shores of secluded beaches, let the spirit of Greece envelop you, awakening your senses and igniting your sense of wonder. Whether you're marveling at ancient temples, basking in the warmth of the Mediterranean sun, or dancing under the stars to the rhythms of bouzouki music, Greece casts its spell upon you, leaving an indelible mark on your heart and soul.

So, as you bid farewell to this enchanting land, carry with you the memories of sun-kissed days and starlit nights, the laughter of new friends and the whispers of ancient spirits. For in Greece, the journey never truly ends—it lives on in the stories we share, the dreams we dare to dream, and the longing in our hearts to return once more to this timeless land of myth and magic.

Made in United States
Orlando, FL
16 June 2024